Dreams for Kids

*Changing the World
One Person at a Time*

TOM TUOHY

ISBN 978-0-615-36818-4

Library of Congress Control Number: 2010927373
Library of Congress Cataloging-in-Publication Data
Tuohy, Tom.
Dreams for Kids / Tom Tuohy. - 1st ed.

Cover Design: Ryan Turek, Tris3ct

Graphic Design: Devyani Seth

Published by:
Dream Vision Publishing
155 N. Michigan Avenue, Suite 700
Chicago, Illinois 60601
Phone: 1-866-729-5454

Contact the publisher for information regarding
special discounts for bulk orders.

Dedicated to
Patricia Tuohy
For all you were and for all you will always be

Praise for
Dreams for Kids

"*Dreams for Kids* captures the true embodiment of humanity. This book inspires people to seek out the 'extraordinary in everyone they meet…to create a world, one community at a time, that embraces all races, economic classes, cultures, and abilities—realizing we are nothing without each other and that we all have value…

Dreams for Kids is a vision of beauty, conviction, and discipline…a way of life…This book brings honor, and character and chivalry back to a culture in desperate need of purpose and meaning."

— Shawna Egan
President/CEO Children's Autism Center

"*Dreams for Kids* has inspired me to do all I can to use my success to lift the lives of at-risk youth. This is something I want to be part of, helping kids, making sure they have good role models. You reach out and you might touch one of these kids and they might want to do the same for another person."

— Pierre Thomas
New Orleans Saints, 2010 Super Bowl Champion

"In a world of great diversity this amazing book will inspire you to truly make a lasting difference in our time and will provide you with a roadmap to personal fulfillment and true success."

— David Herro
CIO, Oakmark International Fund
Morningstar's International Stock Fund
Manager of the Decade

"*Dreams for Kids* is a powerful book of true love and compassion that does not focus on a person's disability, but rather his or her ability.

This book is a living example of the real power of giving and exemplifies the words of Easter Seals founder Edgar F.Allen, who said in 1922, *You have but one life. We get nothing out of that life except by putting something in it. To relieve suffering, to help the unfortunate, to do kind acts and deeds is, after all, the one sure way to secure happiness or to achieve real success. Your life and mine shall be valued, not by what we take…but by what we give.*"

— F. Timothy Muri
President, CEO Easter Seals, Metropolitan Chicago

"There is so much to praise about this book. You will find yourself moved to emulate the examples of decency and dignity that grace these pages, and be inspired to serve others who may not have been so blessed."

— Sam Horn
16 time Maui Writers Conference Emcee
Author of *POP!* and *Serendestiny*

"*Dreams for Kids* demonstrates the power each of us has within us to briefly brighten, if not permanently enhance, the lives of those facing severe limitations—be those economic, physical, genetic, or developmental. "Limitations" is probably not the right word as Tom Tuohy demonstrates that what seems impossible is, in fact, readily achieved when we bring together our creativity and commitment to the belief that anything is possible.

If you don't go to sleep dreaming about where you fit in, it's probably because you're still awake reading it."

— Jack Ryan
President/CEO Little Friends, Inc.

"*Dreams for Kids* is a remarkable work...a story of courage and fear...about strategies for living everyday life with compassion, acceptance and love. One person can truly make a difference and change lives—even their own—by reaching out to those in need."

— John Kemp
Past President, US International Council on Disabilities,
1991 Horatio Alger Distinguished American

"*Dreams for Kids* is one of the greatest diversity and inclusion books I have ever read...stories of ordinary people making an investment in humanity...corporate leaders will greatly benefit from this book."

— Michelle Thomas
Director of Global Diversity, William Wrigley Company

"It is hard to remember when I read a book that hooked me from page one, and did not let me put it down until I devoured every word. This book touched me on so many levels. *Dreams for Kids* is a book about the power of love...love that does not distinguish between giver and receiver...Tom Tuohy clearly knows that power and speaks about it with such unflinching honesty, I found myself unable to look away.

As a culture, our attention drifts too often to what is wrong about the world. Reading this book will remind anyone about all that is right."

— Andrea Patten
Author, *What Kids Need to Succeed,*
Four Foundations to Adult Achievement

Contents

Back to the Future

Dreams for Kids

Preface

You must be the change you wish to see in the world.
~ Mahatma Gandhi

One person can make a difference and create lasting change in the world. Your impact on a single person can result in a ripple effect felt far and wide.

This is the true story of Dreams for Kids. It is a story of hope, empowerment, and transformation.

Dreams for Kids began at the request of my mother, and was influenced by mentors who have empowered millions of young people in communities around the world. These extraordinary humanitarians have changed, even saved, entire communities. They serve as an enduring example of how one person truly can make a difference in our world and produce an astounding living legacy.

You might wonder what you possibly could do to make a significant difference. This book will remind you that your contribution can make all the difference in the world.

We all have felt the pain of isolation. We all have lost someone. By recalling those moments when we feel most alone we can relate to kids who feel this way every moment of their lives. And then we can do something. In reading stories of at-risk young people who have been given opportunity and used that gift to help others, we are filled with hope and the inspiration to place our own lives in perspective. Most importantly, we are motivated to engage and make our contribution, and truly be the change we wish to see in the world.

Within this book is also a new model of engagement, one that will end the isolation of a generation of young people living in poverty, or with disabilities, and engage them as leaders in a new world.

There is courage and determination in this book and there is a common thread that connects every single one of us to it. It is the reminder that we all matter and that the greatest change can come from the most unlikely source.

If there is a lesson, it is that we do have the vision to see past our perceptions, and that limitation is a state of mind. This book is a reminder to each of us that it is through giving that we experience our greatest prosperity. We can learn these lessons from a generation of youth born of destiny, committed to being united, and determined to transform the world.

During one of the most challenging times in human history, when so many people are seeking a sense of fulfillment and a reason to hope, this book gives us the inspiration we need to act and do our part…one person at a time.

1

Kiss of a Dolphin

When you were born, you cried and the world rejoiced.
Live your life so that when you die, the world cries and
you rejoice.

~ Cherokee saying

At the end of the 1980s, with a group of friends, I founded Dreams for Kids, which provides empowerment opportunities for at-risk and isolated youth. For seven years, we focused exclusively on serving youth who lived in severe poverty or had suffered sudden hardship. We took them to events, held parties, and gave them hope. We did whatever we could to give kids who had lost so much the opportunity to be engaged and to know someone cared.

When the organization was in the midst of its seventh year, I read a newspaper article given to me by one of our Board members about a remarkable young man named J.J., whose story not only impacted me personally, but broadened our Dreams for Kids' mission.

I will go into more detail about those beginning years later in the book, but for now, I simply want to tell you J.J.'s story.

J.J.'s Story

In 1995, J.J. O'Connor was a high school senior and hockey player enrolled at Loyola Academy in Wilmette, Illinois. At age sixteen, hockey was J.J.'s passion. With considerable talent, the only drawback was his height. He was rather short, but played with skill and dedication, and excelled in every aspect of the game.

October 24, 1995, began much like any other day for J.J. His hockey team, in Chicago's Class AA midget-level, was scheduled for its first game of the season that afternoon. During the game, he and a friend from the opposing team went for the puck in a corner of the rink. J.J., who had played hockey since he was four-years-old, attempted to duck under his opponent and tripped.

J.J.'s skates had gotten tangled with his opponent's skates and he sailed through the air. As he described that moment, he recalled feeling like Superman—until he hit the boards head-first. Then, he quickly realized that he could only *wish* he were Superman. "I immediately lost all feeling on the way down and never felt anything, even as I hit the ice," J.J. recalled. "I remember looking for my hand and it appearing to be on the other side of the rink because I could not feel it."

"When my head hit the boards, I knew right away that I was paralyzed. It was like everything was leaving my body. When I saw my hand, it was like it wasn't part of my body."

J.J. was taken off the ice on a stretcher and was rushed by ambulance to the emergency room at Evanston Hospital. "I was kind of excited to get into the ambulance. I had no idea this was a life-changing event."

He had fractured three vertebrae. J.J.'s neck and head were fastened to a protective halo, and after surgery to stabilize his spine he would remain flat on his back, for days, then weeks, then months.

He spent nearly three weeks in intensive care, and then he was moved to the Rehabilitation Institute of Chicago, where he stayed for two months. J.J. was transferred to Marianjoy Rehabilitation Hospital, where his hospitalization and intensive therapy continued for seven more months.

When Centimeters Count

That year, J.J. was one of seven hockey players nationwide who broke their necks while on the ice. This was an alarmingly high number of paralyzing injuries, compared with the average of one to two such injuries in a year.

The incredible nature of paralysis is that an injury a quarter centimeter higher or lower on your spinal column can translate into completely different results. When an able-bodied person tells you that he or she has broken their neck or back, they may or may not know just how fortunate they were. When a bone is fractured along your spinal column it comes with extreme risk.

Our spinal cord is the main pathway carrying information from our brain to all the muscles in our body. The spinal cord is protected by vertebral bones and extends from the base of our brain to approximately a few inches below our waist. The tunnel of stacked vertebral bones is called our spinal column. The cord consists of a bundle of nerves called neurons, which carry the messages back and forth to the brain.

When we move our finger or our leg, it is this amazing neurological superhighway that makes it possible, even without conscious thought.

Even the slightest fracture to the protective vertebrae can lead to disastrous results. If the vertebrae impact the spinal cord in any way, even by a slight bruise, the neurons are damaged and paralysis occurs. The signals in our brain that command our movement are unable to reach the muscles.

The amount of paralysis is determined by two factors: the location and the severity of the damage to the spinal cord. The higher the location of injury to the spinal cord, a greater proportion of the body will be affected. A fracture to the high neck area, as with the late Christopher Reeve, can affect the entire body and respiratory system. The difference between a paraplegic (someone who has lost the use of his or her legs but maintains upper body movement) and a quadriplegic (someone who has lost the use of his or her arms and legs) can be just a fraction of a centimeter.

J.J.'s fracture occurred in his neck, at C3, C4 and C5 vertebrae. A fragment of his C4 vertebrae pushed against his cord, and the cord reacted, as did his immune system and the rest of his body. J.J.'s cord was badly bruised, but not cut.

The functionality of someone with a C4 spinal cord injury, such as J.J., is typically limited to full head and neck movement depending on muscle strength, with limited shoulder movement, resulting in paralysis of full upper and lower body. Generally, this also means no finger, wrist or elbow flexion or extension.

If J.J.'s cord had suffered a C5 injury, he would still have use of his arms and might still even be able to drive a car. A C3 injury to his cord would have resulted in him being on a ventilator.

J.J. has been diagnosed as an "incomplete quadriplegic," which means he has some feeling and movement throughout his body. However, all routine daily tasks, from the kitchen, to the bathroom, and even to tying his shoes, require assistance. J.J. requires 24-hour care.

A person with an injury such as J.J.'s requires total assistance, when transferring from a bed to a wheelchair and from a wheelchair into a car. For many individuals with a spinal cord injury, rehabilitation becomes a lifelong process. It takes months, and sometimes years, of learning and practice for a patient to physically manage paralysis; yet it often takes much longer to emotionally accept his or her life as a person with a disability.

Puerto Vallarta, Here We Come

*Most of the time I don't have much fun. The rest of the
time I don't have any fun at all.*

~ Woody Allen

J.J.'s story doesn't stop there. He has become a central figure
in the Dreams for Kids' story. In fact, I will share many J.J. stories
in this book because they are a great source of inspiration.

For now, I want to jump ahead to one of my favorite J.J. stories because it represents the old adage that, "fact is much more
amazing than fiction." The following story also introduced our
organization to a spirit which defines the capacity and privilege
each of us has to reach out and connect with those in need.

After a long and determined rehabilitation, J.J. recovered
sufficiently to finish high school and to attend college. In his
junior year of college, J.J. asked me if I would like to join him on
a trip to Puerto Vallarta, Mexico. It was now four years since we
first met, and during that time we became good friends. He was
introduced to the world of Dreams for Kids and, over time, I was
introduced to the world that fate had given him.

The purpose of this trip? Spring Break, of course!

I had become accustomed to doing whatever I could to
assist J.J., as he attempted to adapt to his new life. We had traveled many a mile, so to speak, but this request was altogether
different. In trying to gather all the enthusiasm I could muster, I
could not help but think of where we would be going and why.

Thankfully, I did not give much thought to the logistical
difficulties of traveling to another country with J.J. I was too worried about returning to college Spring Break after twenty years.
J.J. was concerned that his friend, Dick Marak, would not be able
to negotiate everything that Mexico could pose and thought it
would help for me to come since I had been there several times.

Why not expand our horizons? J.J. routinely expanded his
and has inspired others to do the same. We decided we were

up for the challenge. Foreign country? Spring Break? Here we come! Twenty years later, it was back to the future.

Dick and I decided we would do everything to help ensure that J.J. had the complete Spring Break experience. We were committed to having fun and were especially committed to seeing to it that J.J. had access to anything that the rest of the able-bodied student crowd enjoyed.

Have you ever been on Spring Break? Or have you seen it on TV? Of the thousands upon thousands of students who arrive from across the world, have you noticed that there is a shortage of kids in wheelchairs? There are reasons behind the fact that, of the many students who live with a severe disability, few are ever seen at the most visible of events.

Accessibility for those with disabilities is a problem, which has lessened somewhat over time, although getting around Mexico certainly proved to be a challenge.

However, even with the opportunity for increased mobility and access, for a young person who has a disability, it is more the difficulty of fitting in that limits them. People tend to stare at those in wheelchairs and rarely initiate social contact. As J.J. has shared, it is unpleasant, to say the least, to be ignored and even talked about as if he was not even present.

Another significant challenge for a quadriplegic is that there is an inability to protect oneself. If a car door suddenly opens in front of J.J., he cannot step aside and avoid it. If he sees something falling from above, aiming toward him, he cannot even lift a hand to protect himself. Immobility can be truly frightening.

An Excellent Adventure

Remember what Bilbo used to say: It's a dangerous business, Frodo, going out your door. You step onto the road, and if you don't keep your feet, there's no knowing where you might be swept off to.
~ J.R. Tolkien, *The Lord of the Rings*

Dick and I considered the many challenges we would face on the trip. Dick's attitude was, and always is, "Let's go for it." I couldn't have agreed more. This, however, was in direct conflict with my recurring thought of just what the heck I was getting myself into.

The challenges began at the airport. Do you think air travel is a bit inconvenient? Can you imagine if you were a quad? Add to that, a late arrival at the airport, a last-minute passport challenge and a final announcement that our plane was boarding. Yikes. Picture the three of us running and rolling to the gate. The last gate, of course....

We finally arrived; drenched with sweat and out of breath, to a terminal so far away it might as well have been in another zip code. Once at the gate, we were rather rudely welcomed to "Flying with a Disability 101."

That means you are the first or the last one to board the plane. Those are your only two choices. We, of course, had no choice. Everyone else was already on the plane and quite settled in. J.J.'s wheelchair was taken and stored somewhere else, and we were left with the adventure of figuring out how to get to our seats. Dick never hesitated. He flipped J.J. over his shoulder like a sack of potatoes and headed down the jet-way tunnel. He jogged onto the plane and down the narrow aisle with J.J. hanging upside-down over his back, giving new meaning to the phrase, "carry-on."

Have you ever been the very last person to board a plane? Every single set of eyes is on you. Everyone's eyes are looking over the seats and leaning into the aisles. Most of those eyes aren't very kind, as they perceive you are the one holding up the flight.

Dick simply stopped at our assigned row, and pivoted around to prepare to bring J.J. down into his seat. At which point, J.J., still over Dick's shoulder, picked up his head, smiled at all the eyes, and said, "Sorry to keep you waiting."

I sat down and thought, "Oh boy, this is going to be one interesting week." Little did I know this thought would prove to be the understatement of all time.

Breaking the Ice

One never reaches home, but wherever friendly paths intersect the whole world looks like home for a time.

~ Herman Hesse

Once in Mexico, we headed to wherever the action was. It was always fun to see the look on the taxi driver's face when he pulled up. The driver would usually look at the wheelchair, look into the back seat of his cab, and by the time he looked back at us, Dick had the J.J. sack of potatoes over his shoulder again and onto the front seat. Then Dick would ask for the trunk to be opened, fold up the wheelchair and put what fit inside. Before the driver could say a word, the bungee cord came out of Dick's back pocket to hold the trunk lid down and we were ready to roll again.

Whether it was the market, the beach, a dance floor, or a party in progress, we made the scene. We kept it up, and in a matter of days, everyone in town was familiar with J.J.

I will never forget the first time our taxi pulled up to the largest, open air, student bar in Puerto Vallarta, with students stacked on top of one another, inside and out. Now here comes the taxi with the wheelchair hanging out of the back. By the time the kid on the front seat of the taxi ends up in the wheelchair, there was a shift in the party atmosphere.

As often happens, when J.J. first entered the bar, those people who did not stare, simply looked away. No one responded to him. If it weren't for the help of others, breaking that ice would have taken a sledgehammer.

Luckily, we brought the sledgehammer and his name was Dick. With Dick leading the way, we would simply initiate the conversations and answer the questions that were on most people's minds anyway.

J.J. would be right there, without any reservation, and before anyone could figure out why they were uncomfortable, they realized that this was just another college kid.

Then J.J.'s personality would take over and he would go from being invisible to being the life of the party. J.J. has plenty of personality and charisma to carry a crowd. However, like most people living with a disability, he needed the path of resistance cleared by having friends treat him like he was one of the gang—which he is.

Once you notice J.J. for who he is, and not for what he is sitting in, and you talk to him, his engaging personality and upbeat attitude take over and you're hooked. Actually, as the remainder of the ice melted away, when J.J. rolled in, the competition got a little tougher for the other guys. Young women would be drawn to him for reasons that had nothing to do with the chair. Then, as Dick would say, it is every man for himself. It was always fun watching J.J. and Dick compete for the same girls. In case you are wondering, and almost everyone does, his accident did not take away everything. With effort, the right partner, and the right conditions, J.J. would be, in his words, "good to go."

J.J. soon became the talk of the town. At the pool, if everyone were swimming, we would get J.J. an inner tube. We would then kind of wedge him in the tube, making sure he wouldn't fall through and drop to the bottom of the pool. There, propped up with his head and part of his body above the water, J.J. and his

Ray Bans floated in the middle of the pool and hung out like the rest of the Spring Break kids.

Later in the week, as we were sitting by the pool, a truly great moment occurred. Some girls sitting next to J.J. struck up a conversation. Since we were there first, and helped J.J. into the lounge chair, there was no way of knowing he arrived in a wheelchair. The girls could not tell him apart from any of the other students lounging about in pool chairs which, as you can imagine, is what many people in wheelchairs long for. Just treat me like anyone else. Don't let the wheelchair define me. Don't let the wheelchair intimidate you or scare you away. See *me*. Talk to *me*.

One of the girls asked J.J. if she could borrow our suntan lotion, which was sitting on the table next to me. J.J. said sure and asked me to pass the bottle. Without thinking, I picked the bottle up to hand to J.J. He stared at me, as my arm hung in the air, and J.J.'s hand never left his lap. J.J.'s look said it all, wondering when I was going to remember that he couldn't just grab the bottle out of my hand and pass it to the girl. It finally dawned on me what I'd done. The moment I woke up, J.J., Dick, and I started laughing and could not stop.

It was not the first, nor will it be the last time this type of thing happens. With J.J., it is easy to forget there is anything "different" about him. Aside from the obvious, there is not.

Of course the girl, who is still waiting for the lotion, was wondering what the heck was wrong with us. So J.J., who just got "busted," looked over at her and said with a sly smile, "I wish I could."

That simple moment defined what the three of us had hoped to achieve on this trip. J.J.'s chair had become invisible, to us and to those fortunate enough to meet him.

The amazing event that was about to occur defined the very essence of compassion and acceptance, and our teacher came from the most unexpected of places.

2

Up Up and Away with J.J.

And when the day comes that we can communicate intelligently with dolphins, they may introduce us to the concept of survival without aggression, and the true joy of living, which at present eludes us. In that circumstance what they have to teach us would be infinitely more valuable than anything we could offer them in exchange.

~ Horace Dobbs, *Follow a Wild Dolphin, 1977*

The next morning I was flipping through some tourist brochures, looking for something interesting to do. One ad grabbed my attention. I asked J.J. if he would like to swim with the dolphins at an aquatic facility not far from our hotel. J.J. said he thought it would be "interesting." This was yet another all-time understatement.

If you ever have the opportunity to swim with dolphins, by all means, go for it. According to research, 80% of people who swim with dolphins experience a change in brain wave patterns from beta to theta states of consciousness. This explains why many participants experience states of bliss, ecstasy, deep peace, and a sense of well-being.

We knew little of this, as we rolled past the gates at the facility. Once inside, you don a set of headphones and actually listen to the dolphins communicate with one another. Their capacity for language is well developed. Their clicking sounds are the way they communicate emotions and thoughts to each other. It was breakthrough research by Dr. John C. Lilly, which proved that dolphins, with larger brains than humans, have a complex capacity to communicate.

Interestingly, the actual process of dolphin communication and visual awareness does not involve their eyes, but instead is accomplished through listening. Dolphins create a visual picture of their surroundings by sending out sound waves, or sonar, and receiving them back. This channel of communication creates a virtual reality, something humans are incapable of experiencing without the aid of a computer.

According to the Dolphin Research Unit, dolphin sonar is four times more powerful than the ultrasound or CAT scan used in medical diagnostics, and is more complex than any man-made technology.

As further evidence as to how much more advanced dolphins are at communicating than their human counterparts, consider this: When each dolphin is sounding a visual picture and understanding of its surroundings relative to another dolphin, there is a distinct taking of turns. The receiving dolphin is still, attentive, and always silent while the other speaks. This made me think that a lot of couples could sign their spouses up for dolphin lessons!

The Extraordinary Nature of Dolphins

I never expected to encounter such an abundance of dolphins. Hundreds surrounded our boat, leaping, clicking, making love all around us. They stayed with us for hours sharing their world with ours. The experience of abundance, freedom and pure joy had an inspirational effect on my life.

~ Alex Fisher, *Kindred Spirit Magazine*

When a human enters the dolphin's domain, whether it is a small-contained area or in the vast open waters of the ocean, the dolphin must first adjust to this person. It is always the dolphin's choice to come to you, but only when the dolphin is ready. The dolphin, with its wide-ranging set of emotions, is opening itself up to another living creature.

Consider a stranger across the dance floor that comes up to you and asks you to be his or her partner for a slow dance. You may be able to physically comply, but you would probably need to undergo some emotional preparation to first decide if you wanted to override your natural need for space and your preliminary suspicion of a stranger.

Dolphins are much the same. Close contact for them requires an emotional adjustment. Most humans have no idea that these capabilities are even present.

Because of their ability to "read" one another, as well as other living creatures, the dolphin is so highly developed that they can discern variances in human emotion and physiology. Whether we are kind or aggressive, patient or irritable, fearless or fearful, or a mix of those or any other of numerous emotions, dolphins can detect it.

In Mexico, our group of ten people was carefully "prepped" before we entered the water. We were told that the dolphins would be coming from the far side of the pool. Upon entering the pool, each dolphin would quickly swim along the pool's perimeter, in front of us. We would remain still and allow the dolphins to become familiar with each of us.

During this brief sweep of the pool, each dolphin, by use of its sonar, instantaneously assesses everyone in the water so that the dolphin can feel safe and can make the choice of interacting.

Close Encounters of the Unforgettable Kind

Is there ever any particular spot one can put one's finger and say, 'It all began that day, at such a time and such a place, with such an incident?'

~ Agatha Christie

Dick and I were standing in the waist deep water at the far end of the pool, holding J.J. upright between us. Ten other people were standing along the sides of the pool, stretching from one end to the other. As the first dolphin, a female, entered from the near side, she quickly swept around the perimeter of the pool, directly in front of each person. When the dolphin reached us, she stopped on a dime, right in front of J.J. She became visibly agitated. She shifted quickly from left to right and began to move away, but swept back around toward us and grazed J.J.'s legs. His legs didn't move. The dolphin knew something was wrong.

The dolphin sensed that J.J. was markedly different from the other visitors in the pool. Could she understand that J.J. had suffered physical trauma, perhaps even that he did not have complete neuron function? Did she detect the hardware in his spine, which was used to fuse his fractured vertebrae together? She may very well have understood all of it. Yet, she clearly did not know how to respond.

J.J. knew something was wrong. He quietly asked Dick and me, "Take me out of the pool so I won't ruin it for everyone else."

I will always be grateful for the trainer, who was determined to allow the situation to unfold. He commented that the dolphin was probably just nervous because there were so many people in the water. His reassuring tone made J.J. feel more comfortable and willing to stay in the pool.

The trainer suggested that the attendants bring in the dolphin's mate to help keep her calm. So the male dolphin entered the pool, swept around once, and yes, stopped right in front of J.J. For a few seconds, the male dolphin did not make a move. He was completely still while he seemed to study J.J. Then, he turned and swam to the far side of the pool where the female dolphin joined him. They lingered there for a moment, communicating back and forth.

With everyone completely mesmerized, J.J. turned his head toward me and said with a small grin, "Who do you suppose they're talking about?"

The female dolphin then very calmly moved, alone, to the center of the pool. The trainer asked Dick to take J.J. to the dolphin. As Dick helped J.J. stand upright, the dolphin moved closer to him, slowly rose out of the water, opened her fins, put them around J.J.... and kissed him.

Blessed by a Dolphin

The service we render others is the rent we pay for our room on earth.

~ Sir Wilfred Grenfell

As you can imagine, we were all stunned. J.J. couldn't stop talking about what the dolphin had done. "That was the most amazing thing that ever happened to me," he would later say.

We all understood that what had just taken place was a metaphor for J.J.'s life. "At first, the dolphin was nervous and unsure of me and didn't know what to do. Then, someone helped her understand and see that I was "okay." Then she was able to accept me."

This was such a dramatic realization and defining moment. It would be an enduring example to us all. That dolphin had demonstrated the capability we all have to meaningfully impact someone's life in a moment of grace.

In the world of someone who has a disability, one able-bodied person can set a precedent for everyone else to view that person as a fellow human being, first and foremost. One able-bodied person can help others see past someone's disability and connect with that individual as a person. One person can reach out to another person in need and can change their life.

I have come to see the people who choose to extend themselves in this way as *dolphins*. Dolphins are those individuals who reach out to one and all. Dolphins are those who are committed to contributing to society, to giving back and paying rent for their time on earth.

As we were leaving the pool that day, the male dolphin had yet another gift for us. If the female had captured our hearts, now the male dolphin would soon touch our souls.

Just as Dick and I were helping J.J. from the water, the male dolphin stopped as he was leaving the pool at the far side, turned and swam right up to us. He gently nudged up against J.J. and opened his eyes and looked directly toward him. As J.J. said later, "I will never forget his eyes and the way he looked right into mine. I felt his spirit and it was as if he was saying to me—*you're going to be o.k.*"

Up, Up and Away

I succeeded because you believed in me.

~ Ulysses S. Grant

After the dolphin's kiss, J.J. was ready for more adventures. From our hotel room balcony, we had seen parasailors zip through the sky over the shore. For the first few days, J.J. had not expressed any interest in joining them. Can't imagine why. Inspired by his encounter with the dolphins, however, he was now ready for anything.

As soon as J.J. opened his eyes the morning following his memorable dolphin encounter, he said, "Let's go parasailing."

So, down to the beach we went. After signing one form after another and paying up, J.J. was ready for his next challenge. Well, maybe not so ready. As his time grew closer, sitting in his chair with a life jacket strapped on him, he began second-guessing whether this was such a good idea. I reassured him that it was a good idea; after all it was *his* idea. That bit of reassurance sounded good enough at the time.

When the boat arrived, a crowd gathered as word spread that J.J. was actually going to do this thing. He was going to let this boat pull him out of his chair and into the sky. I could see the fascination. The spectacle of parasailing seems mildly insane to people when they watch an able-bodied person being lifted from the safety of solid ground by a rope attached to a rickety old boat. But from a wheelchair?

Finally, J.J. shrugged and said with a grin, "What the heck, it's not like I have to worry about breaking my neck."

Dick and I lifted J.J. from his chair and stood him up in the sand. We figured that we would sit him on the wooden plank that was attached to the end of the parachute ropes, and stabilize him until he was lifted into the air. We would just hold him up until the parachute opened and he would rise majestically into the sky.

The best laid plans. Nothing like that happened. Not even close. We had not even finished discussing our strategy when the boat simply took off.

J.J. came off the seat, out of our arms, and down onto the beach. His legs dragged along the sand, then along the water and he headed straight for deeper ocean. Dick and I just stood there frozen. Dick looked at me and said, "Oh man, if 'J' makes it back, he's going to kill us!"

Then we ran forward, but the boat continued to accelerate; the line straightened and started to lift him off the water. He was going up! It wasn't graceful and it sure was not what we had planned, but it happened. Boy did it ever happen.

As he rose higher and higher in the air, the sight was majestic.

J.J. was soaring like an eagle. Everyone on the beach was looking up as J.J. sailed across the beaches of Puerto Vallarta, high above the resorts. We could only imagine how exhilarating it must have been for him to soar through the air, as his wheelchair sat empty in the sand.

When the parachute began its descent, all too soon, Dick and I were determined to get this part right. We raced to the spot where J.J. was to land and got there just in time to catch him for a reasonably smooth landing.

Just then a local woman ran up between us, hugged J.J., and with tears running down her face said, "You were so beautiful. Was it scary for you up there?"

J.J. said, "No Ma'am, it's scary down here. Up there I was free."

J.J. found his freedom in the sky, high above Puerto Vallarta and he found acceptance in the magical embrace and kiss of a dolphin.

Dreams for Kids would soon find ways to free other children from the isolation and confinement of their disabilities. However, none of this would have been possible without the mentors whose earlier influence helped shape Dreams for Kids.

One of those great teachers was a man who became a legend by finding freedom for children who were isolated by poverty.

3

Jesse White Tumbles into Our Lives

If you want to lift yourself up, lift up someone else.
~ Booker T. Washington

C abrini-Green is known as one of the world's most notori-
ous and infamous housing projects. Built over a twenty-
year period, between 1942 and 1962, Cabrini-Green was named
for Frances Cabrini, an Italian-American nun who served the
poor and who was the first American to be canonized. The housing project was comprised of over 2,500 living units in a mix of
high-rises and row houses, all tightly contained within several
city blocks.

The area in which Cabrini-Green was constructed, on the
near Northside of Chicago, was once known as "Little Sicily,"
since it was predominantly populated by Sicilian immigrants. In
the early years of Cabrini-Green, the housing was integrated,
with the majority of its residents primarily of Italian descent.

After World War II, the nearby factories closed and thousands of jobs were lost. A shortage of funds resulted in the city

cutting back almost all essential services to the Cabrini project, such as routine building maintenance, area transit, and police patrols. Buildings were neglected. Elevators broke down and pipes burst. Empty apartments were simply boarded-up, lawns were converted to concrete slabs, and in response to the trag-edy of children falling from ill-advised exterior porch galleries, the high-rises were "caged" in with fortress-like mesh across the entire facade, giving the outward appearance and the inside feel of a prison.

Rapidly, there was an exodus of residents who could afford to move elsewhere. The result was that only the most desperately poor residents remained in Cabrini, with 93% living far below the poverty level by the mid-1950's.

Soon, gangs formed and literally controlled individual buildings. Crime was rampant amid the frequent sounds of gun-fire from snipers, resulting in two Chicago police officers being gunned down in broad daylight and a six-year-old boy being killed while walking to school holding his mother's hand.

Residents were afraid to leave their homes, even though their apartments were infested with cockroaches. Buildings were overrun by rats feasting on rotting garbage left to pile up in trash chutes, at one time as high as fifteen floors.

A well-intentioned plan for public housing followed by a series of mistakes and sustained neglect, resulted in an unparal-leled public housing disaster.

Imprisoned within the hopeless confines of the "Greens" were thousands of innocent children, none given so much as a glimmer of hope of escaping the endless cycle of poverty, gangs, and crime.

Just blocks away from Cabrini-Green, past the famed Rush Street nightclub district frequented by the likes of Frank Sinatra, lay the sprawling Gold Coast and Magnificent Mile, an area considered to be the second wealthiest urban neighborhood in the United States. The Gold Coast and Cabrini-Green shared the same zip code, but were worlds apart. Just over the river from Cabrini was the Kennedy Expressway, the route to O'Hare Airport and the suburbs, and visible to the very near south was downtown Chicago. Surrounded by endless prosperity, Cabrini-Green was an island of despair.

Destiny's Dream

The real test of a man is not how well he plays the role he has invented for himself, but how well he plays the role that destiny assigned to him.

~ Jan Patocka

In 1955, a part-time Chicago Public School teacher and Chicago Park District gymnastics instructor moved into an apartment located within a few blocks of Cabrini-Green.

That teacher's name was Jesse White. In the mid-1950's he worked as a part-time Chicago teacher because he was also a full-time Chicago Cubs baseball player.

Jesse White was a Chicago high school sports superstar, earning All-City honors at Waller High School in both baseball and basketball. He has been inducted into the Chicago Public League Basketball Coaches' Hall of Fame.

In 1952, when Jesse graduated from high school, Major League Baseball had just opened its fields to African-Americans. When the St. Louis Browns offered him a professional contract, what had at one time seemed to be an improbable dream was now within reach for Jesse White.

However Jesse White Sr. had other plans for Jesse Jr., since Jesse Jr. had also been offered several college athletic scholarships. On his father's advice that no one can ever take away an education, which will sustain you for a lifetime, he turned down the professional baseball contract offer and enrolled in Alabama State University.

Jesse would be credited with bringing the basketball jump

shot to Alabama and to the old SIAC Conference. By the time he took his last shot, Jesse White became an All Conference scoring legend. He was eventually inducted into both the new Southwestern Athletic Conference (SWAC) Hall of Fame and the Alabama State University Hall of Fame.

Jesse was also an All-Conference baseball player in college and upon graduation in 1956, his hometown Chicago Cubs offered him a tryout. Among hundreds of hopefuls, Jesse was one of only six ballplayers signed to a professional contract.

However, once again fate intervened and Jesse was ordered to report to a camp of another kind, after receiving word that he had been drafted into the Unites States Army.

As always, displaying the drive to excel he applied and was chosen, over hundreds of applicants, to be a paratrooper with the U.S. Army's elite 101st Airborne Division, serving under General Westmoreland.

Jesse completed his military service to his country in 1959 and to this day, he speaks of that service with deep pride, duty and honor. The Chicago Cubs eagerly awaited his return from service and Jesse finally reported to the minor leagues.

Blessed with blazing speed, Jesse's talent, work ethic and good nature allowed him to quickly move up the ranks of the minor leagues to the highest level of AAA baseball. The next stop appeared certain to be inside the famed ivy of Wrigley Field.

However, when the expected time came to be called up to the major leagues, Jesse's phone was silent. It seemed the interventions of his past now played a role in his future. Jesse had missed six years of baseball because of attending college and fulfilling his military obligation. Even though the Cubs promised that he would be brought up to the majors, the unwritten rule was to never call up a player as "old" as thirty-two-year-old Jesse White.

The Cubs' decision still haunts their All-Star second baseman, Glen Beckert, who played with Jesse in the minors. Beckert continues to feel today, in what will surely make long suffering

Cubs' fans cringe, that if Jesse White was playing centerfield for the team in 1969, his role could have made the difference in the Cubs winning the pennant.

So in 1962, with a heavy heart, Jesse White closed the door on a young boy's lifetime dream and hung up his uniform for the last time.

A Hall of Fame Life

When one door closes, another opens; but we often look so long and so regretfully upon the closed door that we do not see the one which has opened for us.
~ Alexander Graham Bell

"I would have loved to have played in the major leagues," Jesse said recently. "That would have been a dream come true, but when dreams don't come true, you move on."

Thanks to his father's advice, he had his college degree and an advanced education. He was prepared to move on. The door to "America's Pastime" may have closed for him, but an open door led Jesse White to Hall of Fame contributions toward America's future.

In 1959, prior to his retirement from baseball and after hitting .312 in the Cubs' minor leagues, Jesse spent his off-season teaching and working as a gymnastic instructor, where he was assigned to the Rockwell Gardens housing project. In October of that year, Jesse White would put on a gym show for the residents of that project.

After putting a group of kids from Rockwell through a strict training regimen, nearly 400 people showed up for the scheduled show to witness an exciting tumbling exhibition.

When the show was over, parents flooded the floor to hug their kids and to thank "Mr. White." Those same parents begged him to continue the team, since it was the only thing that kept their kids off the street and had given them a sense of discipline. Jesse agreed to coach the team for another year.

Early in his life, Jesse had made a personal commitment to someday give back to the community. "I wanted to do something to make a difference in the lives of young people," he recalled.

One year led to the next and at the conclusion of each year, Jesse would announce that it was the final year and the parents would beg him to continue. As he remembers, "The kids would come to me with tears in their eyes and say, 'Mr. White, please don't give up the team.'"

Each night, when Jesse would leave Rockwell Gardens, he would return to his apartment. As he drove past the Cabrini-Green projects, he could feel the desperation. He knew in his heart that the kids that lived in Cabrini-Green needed hope and that those kids deserved an opportunity for a better life. It was time for Jesse's team to expand.

The Jesse White Tumblers

I am of the opinion that my life belongs to the community, and as long as I live, it is my privilege to do for it whatever I can.

~ George Bernard Shaw

Jesse became a full-time Chicago Public School teacher when he retired from baseball in 1962. He continued to work in the evenings, as an instructor with the Chicago Park District. In that role he continued the Tumbling program for the kids of Rockwell Gardens and Henry Horner Homes. Soon Jesse accepted a position at Schiller School, located in the heart of Cabrini-Green. There was no way of knowing at that time that this young, intense school teacher would someday become the most revered man in the history of the "Greens," and would give thousands of kids an opportunity to leap from the projects to heights they never before dared dream possible.

Having decided to expand his Tumbling Team to Cabrini, Jesse would find there was no shortage of eager candidates. In fact, word spread so rapidly about his Team that the project's empty lots were soon filled with old mattresses and kids of all ages jumping and flipping night and day, as they dreamed of having a shot at being on the Jesse White Tumbling Team.

It seems there was a new gang in town and this gang wore red. Jesse had purchased red uniforms for his kids. Whenever the team performed, every Tumbler had to be neatly groomed and the uniforms had to be cleaned and pressed. This new gang was a welcome alternative to the dangerous, dead-end street gangs of the projects.

An amazing street rule was soon established. No street gang in Cabrini-Green would mess with the Jesse White Tumblers. Jesse would make sure of that. In his position at Schiller Elementary School he found out everything there was to know about the street gangs, including who their leaders were. Each and every year he put the word out: Leave his kids alone or suffer the consequences.

So began an unwritten treaty between the vicious and often cold-blooded street gangs and the Jesse White Tumblers. The truce was fortified, in large part, because it became widely known that there was hardly anyone in Cabrini-Green that Jesse White had not helped in some way, and that would include the mothers, brothers and grandmothers of the gang bangers. However, not the least of the reasons is that Jesse White can be as serious as a heart attack. Jesse quickly became known in the "Greens," not only as a benevolent patriarch, but also as a strict disciplinarian who commanded respect. In Cabrini-Green even the gang bangers call Jesse, "Mr. White."

Jesse also knew that it did not take much pressure for kids to join a gang in the projects. Most kids who grew up in Cabrini, like most kids living in poverty, lacked the presence of a father and other positive influences in their lives. They also grew up without much opportunity to belong, and a gang often meant brotherhood and identity.

There had never been an alternative to street gangs in Cabrini-Green. But, then again, there never had been anything like the Jesse White Tumblers. There was an understanding that Jesse's kids were trying to make something of their lives. The gangs would not mess with a kid that had a goal. Besides, to mess with Jesse's kids was to mess with Mr. White.

Tough Love

Ask any police officer in Chicago and you'll know the truth of this next statement. With a hard and serious look Jesse White says, "If any of my kids mess up, they will sooner turn themselves in to the police than deal with me."

Knowing well the dangers and temptations of the projects and the constant negative influence which poverty brings, Jesse has developed a code of conduct that is strict, and without exception.

He is well aware that to bring oneself up from the vicious and unrelenting cycle of poverty, and to have an opportunity for a better life, one needs discipline and must embrace the rules of those who have already succeeded.

Being an elite athlete, Jesse also knows discipline cannot be a random exercise. Discipline must be instilled in those who are young, so that they can have the opportunity to become self-sufficient and to develop self-discipline.

The rules of the Jesse White Tumbling Team are clear and strictly enforced: No gangs, no drugs, no alcohol, no smoking, no profanity, and maintain a minimum C average in all school classes. The list continues and includes several unwritten but clearly understood principles: Be punctual, dress appropriately, be neat and clean at all times, never wear any gang associated clothing or jewelry, learn and practice table manners and common courtesy, and always be helpful and polite to others.

Jesse White is painfully aware that there is an African-American stereotype, just as he knows that people will stereotype other ethnic, racial and religious groups. Jesse is clear that his kids will not exhibit behavior that plays into those stereotypes. "People can look at you and see that you are an African-American. I want people to look at my young people and understand that they are not a stereotype of what people might think African-Americans are. My kids conduct themselves like ladies and gentlemen. I want to dispel the myth that African-Americans do not know how to act and do not have anything positive going for themselves. I always want to show that there is another side that people might not know."

Since he is aware that other people's perceptions can limit what kids can accomplish and is also aware of how vitally important discipline and rules are to self-improvement and success in life, Jesse's code of conduct is strictly and swiftly enforced. There may be a second chance, for he believes in redemption, but there will not be a third. For repeat offenders and for those who violate the cardinal rules, such as committing a crime or associating with gangs, there is no second chance. Jesse will help those individuals to get on with their lives, but they will never be associated with his Team again.

For those who adhere to the standards of the Team, there are rewards beyond measure.

Soaring to New Heights

These kids right here, they're going to be mayors and governors and lawyers and artists and social workers and actors. And you're going to reach for the stars, right? You're going to follow your dreams, right?
~ Antonio Villaraigosa

Jesse White has said many times that kids who must live in the projects have most of the cards in the deck stacked against them. He also believes every child deserves an opportunity for a better life and a chance to achieve all they dream possible.

The problem he has witnessed is that the kids who live in desperate poverty have little or no exposure to anything outside their negative environment. It became his mission to provide his kids with those positive influences, which were missing.

Jesse expanded the reach of the Tumbling Team's performances. The Team would travel to neighborhoods across the state of Illinois, to conferences in the best hotels and to professional sports arenas. The kids would always eat after the performances and rub elbows with executives ranging from Coca-Cola to American Airlines, and meet professional athletes and community leaders.

For kids from the projects, it was often the first time that they would interact with a person of another race or ethnic background, and it was always the first time they were around someone who was not poor. The kids would learn first-hand about opportunities that existed for everyone.

Year after year, the Jesse White Tumbling Team expanded and with it, so did the kid's horizons. The Team soon performed hundreds of times every year, in several states across the country. As they broadened their horizons, it became clear to Jesse that more kids could benefit from his program and so he established the Jesse White Scouts and the Jesse White Drum and Bugle Corps.

The demand for the Tumblers created an opportunity to charge a performance fee. Jesse would divide the fee equally among all who performed. He set up a model to teach financial responsibility, stating that one-third of each amount be saved, one-third be given to their families, and one-third kept for the Tumblers to spend.

As Jesse White's vast athletic, social and cultural enrichment program expanded, he would identify areas of concern and create additional programs that would give the kids the positive reinforcement needed for long-term success. The Jesse White Tutoring Program was established, with certified teachers and volunteers providing one-on-one tutoring of team members, assisting them in maintaining the required minimum C average.

The academic success of Jesse's program would bring further opportunities but at the same time would expose further limitations. Program members would graduate from high school and now be prepared to reach the once improbable dream of attending college. Yet resources for this dream were, at that time, extremely limited. Thus began the Jesse White Scholars Program, which provides current and former program members with financial and academic support in preparation for attending secondary education beyond high school. From technology training, to university visits, to college scholarship, the Scholars Program provides the bridge to a life of great promise.

The astounding growth of Jesse's programs would pale in comparison to what the future would bring. No one could have imagined the heights to which the kids from Cabrini-Green would soar. Once confined to a hopeless island of despair, the children of the Jesse White Tumbling Team would soon become citizens of the world.

4

"From the Soul Coast to the Gold Coast"

*Genuine politics—even politics worthy of the name—
the only politics I am willing to devote myself to—is
simply a matter of serving those around us: serving the
community and serving those who will come after us.*

~ Vaclav Havel

I n 1974, the State Representative representing the 13th District
in Illinois had recently retired. The 42nd Ward Democratic
Organization, in charge of choosing a successor, wanted someone who could relate to the constituents, in what was the most
culturally, economically and racially diverse district in Illinois.
The Democratic Party also wanted someone whose reputation
was beyond reproach and who had strong ties to the community.
They did not have to look far.

When Jesse White was approached to fill the vacancy, politics were the furthest thing from his mind and he was not interested. However, like Jesse White's father before him, legendary
Cook County Board Chairman George Dunne had other ideas.

Mr. Dunne, who gave Jesse his first Chicago Park District job and whom Jesse would come to consider his "Godfather," would spend considerable time convincing Jesse of the good he could accomplish for the members of his community and how a political career, in its truest sense, is about public service. Fate intervened once again and when Jesse relented, he became the new 13th District State Representative in Illinois' Legislative Assembly.

Family Matters

Call it a clan, call it a network, call it a tribe, call it a family. Whatever you call it, whoever you are, you need one.

~ Jane Howard

Three years later, when I was nineteen-years-old, I met the man who became my thirty-year friend, mentor, and role model.

I was a freshman at DePaul University in Chicago when Jesse White walked into the law office where I was working as a clerk. He was dropping off papers for a secretary whose son was in training for the Tumbling Team. When I introduced myself, Jesse was everything I had heard, and hoped, he would be. He invited me to visit the Tumbling Team offices in Cabrini-Green and he said to ask for him whenever I made that visit.

When we look back in time at moments that would later prove to be turning points in our lives, these moments might have seemed ordinary as they occurred. Although it was Jesse's future accomplishments that would make him one of the historic figures in our city, he did seem larger than life, even then, to this college freshman.

Having grown up as the youngest of four children and raised by my mother, a single parent, I identified with those who struggled. I also knew, as Jesse had known in his youth, that one day I wanted to do something to make a difference.

I had worked since I was twelve-years-old and watched in admiration as my mother worked two jobs, yet struggled with combined pay that still left us below the poverty level. However, I also grew up on the Northwest side of Chicago, a middle class area. Chicago was also a particularly segregated city and my exposure to the African-American community was limited at best. There was not a single African-American teacher and only one African-American student in my high school. After high school, I was welcomed into communities that had been invisible to me. What I had assumed about poverty would be eclipsed by the shocking living conditions and the struggle of those who lived in the projects.

Being invited into Jesse White's magnificent world of reaching out and impacting the lives of young people in need made a profound impact on me, and was an experience that helped shape my life and chart the course for my future.

I knew at an early age that I wanted to be an attorney. That people would trust and rely upon you, as their counselor, with matters that affected their families and the security of their future, seemed to be a great responsibility and also a great privilege. However, I had been taught that with privilege comes responsibility to give back.

I saw in Jesse White a person who became a politician, not for power or self-interest, but to serve his community. Jesse had made the commitment to help the next generation and his life was elevated because of that decision.

Anytime I would see him, whether it was with the Tumbling Team or at a political event, he would treat me the same way I would come to see him treat thousands of people over the years. You were important to Jesse, and for that moment in time you were the only person in his world.

As soon as I graduated from law school, I asked him if there was anything I could contribute to his programs. When he took me up on the offer, I had the opportunity to get to know the vast operations of the Jesse White Tumbling Team. I soon realized that those operations, with hundreds of performances each year, were basically run out of Jesse's personal checkbook. Every single year, for twenty-five years, he balanced the program's books with an average of $19,000 of his own money. Jesse would shrug and say, "It doesn't matter, it's about the kids."

In the mid-1980's, Jesse was finally convinced that the amazing program he had created could go even further if it was organized to allow others to assist him. Thus began the first Board of Directors of the newly incorporated, nonprofit, Jesse White Tumbling Team. I was privileged when asked to serve on the Board and I continue that responsibility today. People look at me a little strange when I say I was on Jesse's first Board, knowing that the Tumbling Team is nearly as old as I am.

Over the years, the Team has grown in monumental ways, with performances spanning across the world. The Jesse White Tumbling Team has become one of our city's most popular attractions. With appearances in every summer parade, picnic and outdoor event, it is hard to find a person in Chicago who has not seen the Tumblers perform.

The Jesse White Tumbling Team is never to be mistaken for an average entertainment show. It consists of intense, highly disciplined and extraordinarily gifted performers. With all due respect to P.T. Barnum—this is one of the greatest shows on earth.

Every time a performance is witnessed, even by me, and I have seen hundreds of them, the Tumblers bring every person to their feet. The Tumblers begin with a display of athletic moves that are a combination of grace, freestyle and discipline, all under the unforgiving direction of their coach, Jesse White. At the conclusion of a parade of acrobatic flips and cartwheels, there is always the famous grand finale.

With fifteen to twenty red mats stretched out at a carnival, a sports arena, in a banquet hall, on a parade route or in the middle of a picnic, the Tumblers line up, tiniest to the tallest. One by one, they run the length of the mats, flipping through the air in double or triple somersaults. Each of them then positions themselves, shoulder to shoulder, next to the one who had gone before, stretching down the entire length of the mats. Then every Tumbler who follows runs full speed toward the line, and at the last minute, vaults *over* the entire line of Tumblers, arms stretched wide like an eagle, somersaulting over the last Tumbler, landing on his feet, arms extended! There is nothing like the sight of the *final* Tumbler, with music building the crowd into a hand clapping frenzy, coming from out of the shadows and running to vault over the entire Tumbling Team *and* Jesse White. It is, without question, magnificent theatre.

In 1989, soon after Dreams for Kids began, the President of the Illinois Special Olympics called me because he noticed Jesse White was on our Board. Jesse was actually the first person I turned to when creating the organization.

The president said that he knew he was taking a shot in the dark. Would it be possible to ask Jesse if the Tumblers could perform at the Opening Ceremonies of the Illinois Special Olympics? *In two weeks?*

What the president did not know was that Jesse *never* turned down a request, regardless of the obstacles. However, with the schedule he was keeping in both Chicago and Springfield, and in light of the explosive growth of the Tumbling Team's hundreds of performances a year, this was asking a lot. The two-week part had me a little nervous, to say the least.

I called Jesse and he agreed to attend, without hesitation or thought as to his schedule. Over the years, Jesse's secretary has begged me to call her first, because he never looks at his calendar and always says yes. She is running short on miracles.

On the night of the event I was standing in the parking lot of Illinois State University anxiously awaiting the arrival of the Tumbling Team. It was almost 7:00 p.m. Could Jesse have forgotten? Was there a scheduling conflict? He was never late.

Since his days of jumping out of perfectly good airplanes, Jesse remained on strict military time and discipline.

Ten minutes to 7:00 p.m., the Tumbling van, mats tied to the top, filled with twenty kids, came around the corner on two wheels. Calm as could be, Jesse asked, "Where do we set up?" When I told him I was getting nervous, he said, "I would have been earlier but I was in session today, and I had to pick up the kids."

Session! That matter of fact statement meant, that after fulfilling his duties in the legislative session in Springfield, Jesse White drove 200 miles to Chicago, picked up twenty kids, drove 180 miles back to Bloomington and would drive another 180 miles home—all for a *ten minute* show! Seeing the look on my face, he put his arm around me and said something I had heard countless times, "We're family, Tuohy. That's what we do."

A Color Blind View

> *One day our descendants will think it incredible that we paid so much attention to things like the amount of melanin in our skin or the shape of our eyes or our gender instead of the unique identities of each of us as complex human beings.*
>
> ~ Franklin Thomas

What is remarkably consistent about Jesse White is that when he walks out of his apartment every day, he leaves color at home. Your color and his. Jesse refuses to see a person by the color of his or her skin and refuses to let others limit him by something so insignificant. He truly treats every person, from every walk of life and every background, exactly the same.

"I have never used the color of my skin as an excuse or advantage. My parents taught me to love every single person," Jesse said recently.

What is even more incredible about Jesse's view of the world and of his place and others in it is that he has experienced the ugliness of racism and bigotry firsthand, in ways that many will be fortunate never to encounter.

In 1952, Jesse chose to attend college in Alabama. On his first day in, he registered for classes and wanted to go downtown, so he got on a bus and sat right behind the driver. Jesse noticed every single black person on board waving for him to come to where they were sitting—in the back of the bus.

When the bus driver turned around and saw Jesse sitting behind him, he said, "My God! What are you doing here?"

Jesse told the driver that he had paid his fare. The bus driver asked him if he could read the sign, *Colored Seating Behind This Sign.*

He could not believe what he was asked and figured he had paid his fare and could take whatever seat he wanted. So Jesse refused to move to the back of the bus. The bus driver pulled over and left the bus to walk over to a police car, but before he could talk to the officer, a car ran a red light and the squad car took off after it. After the driver returned and the bus reached downtown, the people in the back of the bus gathered around Jesse. They told him in no uncertain terms, that if that police officer had learned what he had done, he would have been locked up and the key thrown away. By the time Jesse got back to school, word had spread throughout campus that this kid from Chicago had refused to sit in the back of the bus.

It was three short years later, on December 1, 1955, that a woman by the name of Rosa Parks also refused to move to a seat in the back of another Montgomery, Alabama bus. Rosa Parks' arrest changed the course of American history. When Jesse graduated the following year, he took any seat he wanted for the bus ride home to Chicago.

Jesse's minister in college was a twenty-four-year-old Reverend, whose name was Dr. Martin Luther King Jr. In 1956, the students at Alabama State College raced to, and surrounded

Dr. King's house, a few blocks from campus, after it was bombed following the historic citywide bus boycott. The Voter's Rights march from Selma to Montgomery would be next. In the years that followed, Jesse was subjected to incidents that now seem hard to believe.

Routinely, Jesse was denied entrance into restaurants and told that he had to eat in the kitchen. One restaurant owner told him that he would be "hung," if he dared step inside.

In his time with the Chicago Cubs, Jesse White was black-listed for *talking* to a white woman reporter. The abuse from the fans, just for being a man of color, was brutal. He was challenged to fistfights, simply because he was a black man wearing a suit and was dressed better than a white man.

Through it all, he never let the actions of others affect his spirit and never let them become part of who he was or how he viewed others. To Jesse, it's as simple as this: once you see the viciousness of racism and experience how it hurts, it should then be easy to eliminate it from your life.

The same principle holds true for his Tumblers. In fact, it is a rule for which there is no exception. Jesse believes that prejudice cuts both ways, "I teach my kids that the 'race card' is the most vicious card in the deck and if they ever play it, then they are off the team."

Maybe it helped that he grew up in an area in Chicago where poor Italian immigrants settled. He learned the customs and language of the Italians and has spent his life embracing the customs of all races, religions and neighborhoods.

Jesse takes the kids into communities as diverse as Irish, Chinese, Jewish, German and Polish. After the performance, the kids will stay to eat with the audience and learn the people's customs. In the middle of it all is Jesse White, speaking the words of the native dialect, dancing a Philippine dance, or teaching the kids how to use chopsticks.

His universal embrace of all people continued in a political career of vast public service that became historic.

Blazing a Trail

I have a dream that my four little children will one day live in a nation where they will not be judged by the color of their skin, but by the content of their character.

~ Dr. Martin Luther King Jr.

Whenever Jesse White visits a restaurant today, he is welcomed with open arms and shown to the best seat in the house. While he enjoys sitting with the owner and impressing him with his vast knowledge of the regional food on the menu, the history of the neighborhood and his awareness of the owner's background and interests, he always spends time in the place where he was required to eat not so many years before. There, beyond the swinging doors, in the kitchen, you can hear the voice of Jesse White surrounded by cooks and dishwashers.

With a personal style that welcomes all, Jesse won admiration, not just from his unique constituents of the 13th District, but beyond its borders as well. Representing both affluent and predominantly white residents of the Magnificent Mile area, as well as African-Americans residents of Cabrini-Green, Jesse White was re-elected and served the community for sixteen years. Jesse describes his fascinatingly diverse district as, *"The Soul Coast to the Gold Coast."*

Jesse's time spent as a State Representative was without compromise. He was there to serve. He chaired the House Human Services Committee, consistently voting and sponsoring legislation that protected labor and human rights. He also served on the select committees on education, children and aging. His Good Samaritan bill became law, and for the first time left-over food from institutional dinners and fundraisers could be given to food pantries and organizations that fed the poor, instead of being thrown out.

In 1992, Jesse was encouraged to run for the county-wide

office of Cook County Recorder of Deeds, an election he won with ease. In 1998, after serving two terms, as Jesse coined it, "The Recorder of your Good Deeds," Jesse White, against all odds, won state-wide office as the 37th Secretary of State of Illinois, the first African-American to ever hold that office. All of Jesse White's good deeds had once again been returned to him, and he would use this larger stage to broaden the base of his extraordinary community service.

The Secretary of State of Illinois is the largest and most diverse public office in the country. Secretary White has used his position to champion the issues which matter most. He has fought hard and won passage of tougher DUI laws and strict uncompromised adherence to handicapped placards. He also hired a former U.S. Attorney as an independent Inspector General, in order to clean up an office that had a vast history of corruption.

He has used the Secretary of State's responsibility for the advancement of literacy programs by: Budgeting over $8 million a year for statewide literacy programs and by creating the Penny Severns' Summer Family Literacy Program, in honor of a political opponent who died of breast cancer.

As Secretary of State, Jesse may be most proud of his advancement of the Illinois Organ Donor Program. Years ago, his sister, Doris, received a kidney transplant which saved her life. Jesse committed to travel the state to encourage residents to sign up as organ donors. To date, he has collected an astounding 6 million donors, leading the nation in organ donor programs.

In November 2002, Secretary White won re-election as Illinois Secretary of State by garnering 2.3 million votes and winning 69.4 percent of the vote total. That was the largest plurality in state history and the largest individual vote total by any Illinois candidate in over a quarter of a century.

In a resounding statement, he won every single of the 102 counties in Illinois, the first African-American to ever do so in Illinois history.

Soaring to New Heights

*Give a man a fish and you feed him for a day. Teach a
man to fish and you feed him for a lifetime.*

~ Chinese Proverb

Throughout his lengthy and celebrated political career,
Jesse has never forgotten his Tumblers. Far from it. He has used
his exposure as an opportunity for his kids to reach greater
heights. With every available moment, Jesse packs the van and
picks up the kids. Performing in places far and wide, Jesse White
has opened doors that few kids ever knew existed.

"It's all about exposure," he explains. "I want these young
people to get out of their environment and see that there is a big,
wide, wonderful world out there. I want them to feel it, touch it
and be a part of it."

Although he was offered the Secretary of State's mansion
in Springfield, he turned it down in favor of the place which
keeps him close to the people; his small apartment across the
street from Cabrini Green.

The Tumbling Office has remained within walking distance of the projects and it is there that Jesse can be found in
his free time, organizing the Tumbler's schedules and practices.
Until a couple of years ago, Jesse personally washed the entire
team's uniforms in the laundry room of his apartment building.
The reason he stopped doing their laundry was because others
finally persuaded him that requiring the kids to clean their own
uniforms would further their lessons in responsibility.

One pursuit that Jesse loves is fishing. In fact, in any vehicle
he drives there must be fishing gear. It will come as no surprise
to learn that he even uses fishing as an opportunity to teach the
kids. If one of the kids is going through a rough period, or Jesse
senses the time is right, off they go to the nearest lake to fish, and
to talk about life.

I remember a few years ago when Jesse waved me down

as I was walking in the neighborhood and said from the driver's side of the Tumbling van, "Get in Tuohy." Within minutes we were in Terry's Finer Foods filling boxes with snacks. Jesse said, "There was an incident at one of the schools and the kids are going to be down about it. We gotta go cheer them up." What is remarkable is that Jesse does things like this all the time and has done so for many years. Recently, he told me that he believes his service to others is an obligation to do good for at least one person every single day. "Each day, if I did not do some good, for at least one person, and most every day it has to be several people, I would not be able to sleep that night."

Jesse's motivation for being such a remarkable humanitarian is, in his words, "No one has gotten to where they are without the help of others. I believe we are required to do the same for the next person."

Knowing that Christmas can be a lonely and hungry time in the projects, Jesse makes it a point to know who is in the greatest need around the holidays. He then personally delivers presents and food. That effort began when he received word one year that twenty-five families would be without a Christmas dinner. Jesse personally delivered hams and turkeys. That was forty-one years ago. Each year Jesse found others who were doing without, at a time when most were celebrating in abundance.

Within a few short years, Jesse was providing and delivering dinner for hundreds, and then, thousands! He realized, as we later did at Dreams for Kids, that there are so many people who are struggling to get by every single day, and Christmas should not be one of those days.

Today, the Jesse White Holiday Fund reaches an astounding number of families. For the last ten years, over 9,000 families have been served each and every year across Chicago. The residents who are served include those living in senior centers and housing complexes. In 2009, beginning at dawn and working through the night with as many volunteers as he could gather, Jesse and crew delivered Christmas dinner for over 10,500 families!

As you might expect, he stays in touch with the thousands of Tumblers who have graduated from his programs, and whose lives he has changed and indeed saved.

The profound effect that Jesse has had, and continues to have, on the children of Cabrini-Green can be felt in and around the neighborhood, and in the lives of those who have gone on to higher education, well paying careers and stable family lives.

Today, when Jesse walks through the Cabrini neighborhood, people stop, remove their hats and shake "Mr. White's hand." He is known by everyone and what he has done for generations makes his presence seem surreal.

To this Jesse would shrug and say, "It's called *la familia*." Once you are welcomed into Jesse White's extraordinary extended family, you are there for life.

Since that night when it all began in Rockwell Gardens, in October of 1959, more than 11,000 kids from eleven communities across Chicago have participated in the Jesse White Tumbling Programs. Fifty years after that first gymnastics show, in the year 2010, the Tumblers will bring 1,100 shows across the world. They have traveled throughout the United States and appeared in nearly every professional sports arena from coast to coast, and have performed at the World Series, the NBA Finals and for nearly every professional baseball, basketball and football team.

The Jesse White Tumbling Team has performed at the White House and for the last three Presidential Inaugural Parades. They have appeared on Good Morning America, the Tonight Show with Jay Leno and Late Night with David Letterman. Members of the Team have also performed and toured with the Harlem Globetrotters and the Ringling Brothers Barnum and Bailey Circus.

Once isolated within the desperate confines of Cabrini-Green, The Jesse White Tumblers have become true citizens of the world, traveling and performing in places as far and wide as Japan, China, Bermuda, Canada, and Jamaica.

For a man whose dream was to play professional major league baseball, and instead, whose destiny blazed a trail of unparalleled community service and dedication to future generations, a chance denied at Cooperstown has given way to a legendary Hall of Fame life.

The man they call "Mr. Cub," baseball great Ernie Banks, says "When I started playing baseball in the Negro Leagues, I looked to Jackie Robinson as a mentor. I continued to look at the qualities of the men I admired and I tried to emulate them. Jesse White is one of those men. He was always a great inspiration to me because of all that he did. I watched what Jesse was doing with those kids and I wanted to give back to the community where I lived. Jesse White is an incredible man, and I have passed on some of his lessons to my children and to other people that have come into my life. Don't forget where you have come from and give something back. Those are the qualities I have learned from being around Jesse."

For thirty years, when anyone wanted to drive to the Gold Coast from the west, it was understood that you drove a mile in either direction instead of driving down Division Street, which cut a path right in the middle of dangerous Cabrini-Green. Today, Division Street is home to new shopping centers and mixed-used housing developments as well as luxury townhouses.

In the few housing project buildings that remain, when the Jesse White Tumbling Team van rolls through the side streets of Cabrini-Green, they pause out of respect for a living legend. All these years later, Jesse White is still driving the van. When the van turns onto Division Street it passes beneath the new Division Street sign, which now bears the name, Honorary Jesse White Way. A street may have been named in his honor, but entire generations live today with hope because of the life of Jesse White.

United States Senator Dick Durbin states, "Jesse White is almost mythical in terms of his reputation. Today the two most popular vote getters in Illinois are Jesse White and Barack Obama. People like Jesse White have laid the foundation for future generations to have a chance…."

When Jesse White's college minister, Martin Luther King Jr., was killed in 1968, it left a generation of African-Americans without a leader and with little hope. In frustration, the days following Dr. King's assassination were filled with riots and the streets of the Westside of Chicago were in flames.

From the smoldering ashes of a desperate neighborhood walked a small Irish priest, who dispensed a message of hope. For the next twenty-five years, this courageous humanitarian would bring his message to the forgotten children of the Westside, and he would lead thousands back to their lost dreams.

5

We Call Him Father Wally

*Be generous, and you will be prosperous. Help others,
and you will be helped.*

~ Proverbs 11:25

I went to college at DePaul University in the late 1970's.
During that time, I was privileged to encounter a man by the
name of Father Walter Brennan, a theology teacher and also a
fraternity moderator. A fraternity moderator is a spiritual counselor who advises the fraternity brothers both collectively and
individually, particularly when they have gone astray. On occasion, some of our brothers in our fraternity engaged in behavior
that merited a little counseling to say the least.

Father Wally was a well-educated man who kept us
grounded. More importantly, however, he mastered the art of
connecting with others in an unassuming, down to earth way
that made all feel comfortable. Consequently, most people were
shocked to learn that Father Wally had two doctorates, one in
theology and one in philosophy.

As an Irishman from the neighborhood, Father Wally fit the
bill in many ways. He had a quick wit, great skill as a storyteller,

and a wicked sense of humor. Though he earned advanced scholastic degrees, Father Wally came across as a regular guy, with no airs, dispensing his wisdom in a manner not typical of a learned man steeped in the academic world.

Father Wally's innate ability to relate and communicate with others transcended his brilliant work at the university. He was a great teacher. He also possessed the unique and effective way of relating to kids our age. He attended our fraternity parties, had a beer or two, and fit right in. Whenever the fraternity took road trips, such as skiing trips to Colorado, Father Wally would be right there with us. He did not ski and would not participate in some of the more adventurous things we did as college students, but he was as much a part of those trips as anything I now remember. Amazingly, he also attended all of our "Hell Weekends," the annual initiation rites of the new brothers, and most often he provided the only link to common sense and sanity.

Bringing the Mass to the Masses

We think of the effective teachers we have had over the years with recognition, but those who have touched our humanity we remember with a deep sense of gratitude.

~ Anonymous student

Rather than requiring fraternity brothers and friends to attend church services, Father Wally brought his service to us. He would ask one of us to pick up a loaf of bread and a bottle of wine. Father Wally might choose to have mass wherever we happened to be. On campus, he'd say, "Let's go sit on the grass," referring to an open space in the quadrangle. He sometimes conducted mass at our residences, before or after classes, on any day of the week.

It was a privilege and an enriching experience to attend Father Wally's services. Despite his ability to relate to a bunch of knuckleheads like us, he was a deeply spiritual priest. A member of the Marian Order of Servites, Father Walter Brennan was a great scholar of the Scriptures and also a widely respected historian of early Christian literature. His treatises on the Christian faith, and in particular on the Virgin Mary, were published worldwide. Father Wally was often recognized for his eloquent views on the importance of Mary in the history of the Church and is the author of the book, *The Sacred Memory of Mary*.

In a most unique and powerful way, he reached out and connected with us at a level at which we could relate. He taught us the great lessons in life, but at the same time was someone with whom we could both identify and respect. Father Wally dispensed his wisdom to us at an age and time when we needed it the most.

As our spiritual advisor, counselor, and friend, Father Wally's impact was far-reaching and profound. He became a friend to each of us and was someone whose influence remains to this day.

It didn't matter how many years skipped by, Father Wally was always there if you needed guidance or simply wanted to say hello. He celebrated and performed the ceremonies of my fraternity brothers who married and baptized their children. He was there to console us and to preside over the funerals of those we loved, including the funeral of my own mother. If you called or visited him, no matter how many years out of college, that strong, vibrant connection was still there. He was always ready to see you and was always prepared to listen. In my case, now twenty-five years after leaving DePaul University, Father Wally's influence and impact on my life continues to be extraordinary.

While Father Wally was the quintessential dolphin for each of us, his influence reached across the university and beyond, during his more than twenty-five years of service to the DePaul community. During his tenure, Father Walter Brennan was voted, by the entire student body, as the most popular and most respected professor at DePaul University. Quite a distinction, considering DePaul University is the largest Catholic University in the country with over 20,000 students.

A Ministry in the Streets

The ultimate measure of a person is not where they stand in moments of comfort and convenience, but where they stand at times of challenge and controversy. The true neighbor will risk their position, their prestige and even their life for the welfare of others. In dangerous valleys and hazardous pathways, they will lift some bruised and beaten brother to a higher and more noble life.

~ Dr. Martin Luther King Jr.

During his years at DePaul University and as our fraternity moderator, Father Wally chose to live in one of the most economically depressed and dangerous areas in Chicago. He could have lived wherever there was a parish and still teach at DePaul. He chose, however, the most desperate neighborhood in the city. The Lawndale and Westside communities had suffered the most damage following the riots on the days following Martin Luther King's assassination. Many Westside residents lived hard lives, amidst sky-high crime rates, run-down streets, and abandoned buildings. Few residents could escape the cycle of poverty that engulfed the area.

Father Wally was never one to back down from what he thought was a righteous cause. If he felt that something was wrong, he took a stand. He confided in us that he marched with the protestors during the infamous Democratic National Convention in Chicago in 1968. He said he rarely spoke of it for fear of retribution. Father Wally also said that he never regretted marching alongside of the protesters because he knew in his heart their cause was right. When he spoke of that day, he was very quiet. Father Wally seemed to carry sadness for the deep divide that existed during that time and especially for those whose voices were not heard. Father Walter Brennan had a bit of a rebel in him, to be sure, but he rebelled in the most conscientious of ways and always stood on the side of the disenfranchised. It was what endeared him to so many: Father Wally's unwavering support of what was just.

Father Wally was surprised to find that the priests of this inner-city parish, Our Lady of Sorrows, rarely stepped outside its gates. Like some academics that never leave the proverbial ivory tower, the priests of this historic parish had little contact and no real connection with the surrounding neighborhood. The priests who lived in the rectory never left the parish walls to involve themselves in the neighborhood, or to even visit with their parishioners. This was something that Father Wally could not understand. The term "parish" meant neighborhood and community to him.

When Father Wally asked his fellow priests why they did not circulate within the community, the response was uniform: It is too dangerous out there. Father Wally felt that the community desperately needed the priests to walk among them for that very same reason, and he decided to force the issue. Hence, this remarkable scholar, teacher, and counselor expanded his ministry to yet another level. He chose to walk the streets of the Westside, alone, and at night.

Father Wally once told me, "I taught during the day and night was the only time I had available. It was also the most important time to be there for the people in the greatest need." So, this very short, unassuming and unfailingly kind Irish priest walked the streets of the desperately poor African-American neighborhood on Chicago's Westside with no sacred or signifying garments, no shield, no special badge, and no indication of privilege or position. Father Wally walked the streets as a simple man, a human being, and most importantly, someone who cared.

At the height of the summer, during intense heat, he would don his Chicago Cubs hat, a simple shirt, black dress socks, shorts so long they almost touched his gym shoes. I told him once that he didn't wear shorts, they were short pants! In the winter it was a parka reaching far below his knees. Fashion was not Father Wally's concern. He didn't care what he looked like; his concern was what he meant to people and how he could be of service. He established a roving ministry. We called Father Wally the Mother Teresa of the Westside.

More than a Presence

Too often we underestimate the power of a touch, a smile, a kind word, a listening ear, an honest compliment, or the smallest act of caring, all of which have the potential to turn a life around.

~ Leo Buscaglia

As a result of his nightly walks and his exceedingly close ties to the community, Father Wally realized as the years passed that his mere presence in the neighborhood wasn't enough. He would tell us that he saw a twelve-year-old boy standing on a street corner, waiting for the bus, wearing a girl's torn shirt, on a freezing cold January night. Asking the boy why he had that shirt on and why he wasn't wearing a coat, the boy responded that it was the only shirt he had and he did not have a coat. So Father Wally took that child to the store and bought him a shirt and a coat. He would perform these kinds of deeds daily, for twenty-five years.

Father Wally would say, "Until you're there, in the neighborhood, you simply don't understand the needs that people face." He would tell us that the extent of the poverty was staggering, and that the toll on the human spirit was beyond measure.

Father Wally said people need hope and in this neighborhood, they were desperate for it. He explained that his assistance could not be a one-time event and he needed to be there on an ongoing basis. He believed it was important to teach those he helped that they could help themselves, and know it was possible for them to have a better life.

Father Wally knew this took money and he had little of it. So he organized efforts to raise funds to provide tuition for the children of the neighborhood so they could realize their improbable dream of going to college. He would buy clothes and food for entire families and provide transportation for countless individuals where none existed. Father Wally initiated two annual fundraisers: a summer picnic and a winter sports memorabilia auction that garnered the strong support of his current and former students of DePaul. Many of our fraternity brothers, now out in the working world, supported his efforts. A magical evening that brought together generations of students, and even their parents, became an annual event to visit with old friends and to support the mission of our mentor. In the spirit of the night, $35,000 to $40,000 was raised to support Father Wally's efforts in the community.

Father Wally dispensed these funds wisely and with a purpose. He used some of the money to offer part-time jobs for people to work in and around the parish. He knew kids could develop a sense of self-worth and motivation if they were offered a real job and were paid for their efforts. Father Walter Brennan searched the streets for those longing for a place in the future, and in the generous soul of a tireless humanitarian, the children of the neighborhood found hope.

Years later, reflecting on his efforts, Father Wally said, "I needed to do this; I had to do this." It was important to Father Wally to make connections with the kids who were simply hanging out. Many of those kids were not the ones who came to church. He felt that maybe he could prevent them from heading into trouble. If they were without critical connections at home, such as having a father present in their lives or having a positive support system, then perhaps he could be a surrogate father or offer a secure environment.

Father Wally opened the parish doors of Our Lady of Sorrows in ways that had never been available in the past. The television room was now a place for the kids to come and watch basketball and football games. The kitchen in the rectory was a place to make a sandwich and enjoy food, which was scarce outside those walls. Now there was an oasis in the neighborhood where kids could gather safely and be surrounded by a positive influence.

If tragedy struck out in the streets, beyond the safety of the parish walls, as it often did, then it was time to be with the people where they lived. In a neighborhood where the sound of gunshots was common, and boarded-up buildings and empty lots made up the landscape, a small priest would step out his front door, alone, to walk among the poor and the forgotten.

A Neighborhood Full of Brennans

To touch the soul of another human being is to walk on holy ground.

~ Stephen Covey

As you might imagine, Father Wally was a humble man. Whenever he had the time to meet and share a meal with former students, there was a single requirement: The meeting could never, ever, be at a "fancy" restaurant. Fancy was the word Father Wally used to describe any place that excluded the common folk. If the restaurant was a place where you had to dress differently and could not be yourself, he simply would not go there.

I was fortunate to meet often with Father Wally for breakfast and the occasional dinner. If I could get him out for dinner, he would request, "that little place, with the good food." He was speaking of a pizzeria in the middle of an inner city block, with three booths and two tables. We regularly met for breakfast, early in the day, and always at a place called Uncle Mike's. Uncle Mike's was the classic American breakfast joint. A counter and a few booths filled with city workers, police officers, mail carriers, neighborhood residents and retirees. A waitress named Sally and a great short order cook named Gus made up the entire staff. Eggs any way you like them, potatoes, and a hot cup of coffee. Father Wally was right at home.

One day, at breakfast, Father Wally told me a story of a young child he met while walking the neighborhood. Over the years, he supported this young man's dream of a life free from the crime of the neighborhood and he offered him the shelter of the parish and gave him positive encouragement. Father Wally was proud of this young man as he went on to graduate from school, marry, and raise a wonderful family. The young man came back to see Father Wally one day and told him that he had two sons who he wished to have baptized. He said he named both of his sons Brennan.

Father Wally laughed so hard telling that story and then said, "You know there are a lot of people named Brennan in the neighborhood now." Father Walter Brennan looked out the window, and for a moment I saw a look of peace and a sense of pride on his face. Just as I was thinking of something good to say to him, he looked back, smiled, and said, "I sure hope all the Brennans are staying out of trouble!"

Father Wally represented so much to me that I constantly sought to reaffirm our deep connection. Simply being around him gave me a sense of contentment and purpose. Of course, he was to become the spiritual advisor and a member of the original Board of Directors of Dreams for Kids.

One day, in the spring of 2001, at one of our early morning breakfasts, I reminded Father Wally that we were not getting any younger and it might be a good time to document his philosophy and approach to community involvement. I asked him, "Why don't you write something that we could use as a guide, so that others could read it and learn what you have accomplished? You could use this as an opportunity to explain the ways you have managed to bridge the gap between blacks and whites. It can be a treatise on how to reach all children of poverty and positively impact their lives."

At first, Father Wally was resistant. He felt that simply reading this information would be a poor substitute to actually being in the neighborhood, walking the streets, and making connections. He believed that the only way one can truly make a difference was to show up every day in the trenches. Trust, in his eyes, came from constant work and affirmation. I fully understood Father Wally's concern, but I also believed that to be able to pass on his wealth of knowledge could only yield a great benefit.

I said to Father Wally that if he could teach people to do what he had done, then more of us could have an impact in the work he had begun. At first he said that this approach would not work because it was about trust. The people in the neighborhood trusted him because he was there everyday and never abandoned them. It worked because he was there.

As our discussion progressed, it proved to be an amazing insight into the depth of Father Wally's knowledge of the cycle of poverty and of race relations. It was a morning I will not soon forget. We talked about the day that was sure to come, when Father Wally was no longer here among us. He began to see the value of leaving something behind.

We both knew that when Father Wally passed on, this poor and mostly forgotten community would lose their champion. The people whom he had given so many years of his life to would be sorely in need of others who cared. Perhaps some others could step in, and the community would trust them because they were Father Wally's friends.

This idea intrigued Father Wally, and it excited him to know that his work might go on long after he was gone. He decided he would write up a plan, a "blueprint." Within this blueprint would be his insights, gained through many years of experience in working with the poor and connecting with people of different races and cultures.

Blueprint for Harmony

> *I believe that there is a plan and a purpose for each person's life and that there are forces working in the universe to bring about good and to create a community of love and brotherhood. Those who can attune themselves to these forces-to God's purpose-can become special instruments of His will.*
>
> ~ Coretta Scott King

About a week later, Father Wally called me at my office and said that he had finished his blueprint. He was going to e-mail it to me. We both laughed because Father Wally was far from being a technological wizard. The kids he helped had recently set up his computer and taught him how to use it. As was his nature, he was both bewildered by the advancements of our time, and excited about learning a new skill. He even planned on taking a computer course so that he could stay current with the times. I can remember the first time he asked to use my cell phone. He had no idea how to use it and held it like a walkie-talkie. As soon as he realized that all the kids in his street ministry had cell phones, he got one too. On his cell phone, he was forever walking and talking, staying in touch, and making a difference.

That afternoon, Father Wally pressed the right button and successfully e-mailed his blueprint to me.

When I received and read his manuscript, I gained new insight into the brilliance of Father Wally. I found the document to be a simple, straightforward, yet profound view into human nature. The blueprint has prescriptions for all of humanity, yet can be applied on the street level.

The blueprint also offers keen insights into what separates individual human beings or groups of people. Father Wally clearly spelled out that it is a lack of understanding that divides individuals, communities, races, cultures, religions, and even nations. From this lack of understanding and ignorance about one another, prejudice is born and it grows, which then further clouds our vision. If we are able to better understand one another, we can begin to bridge the divide that exists between us. We can then tear down those walls and learn to appreciate one another.

In his writing, as in his everyday life, Father Wally pulled no punches. He wrote about the differences between blacks and whites, and why there is so much misunderstanding that exists between the races. He spoke about the characteristics of each group and how, if we were able to focus on those common characteristics, we would find the differences easier to accept.

Father Wally wrote of the fact that almost all of us in this country are descended from some other place. When we begin to understand and appreciate our respective origins and how they impact family and neighborhood, and how collectively we have become the United States, much becomes clear to us. Ultimately, Father Wally wrote a blueprint of understanding and cooperation and of potential harmony among people of all colors.

It was in his deep spirituality that Father Wally held the belief that God works through each of us, and once we understood the suffering that existed among those in great need, we would do God's work here on earth by being generous and kind. In the words and actions of Father Wally, "When you want to help someone, first you have to understand who they are. When you understand who they are, then you can gain acceptance. When they accept you in their life, they will trust you. When they trust you, you can truly make a difference."

The full text of Father Wally's brilliant blueprint and extensive insights on race relations and his work with the members of the Lawndale and Westside communities of Chicago is available in its full edited text on the Dreams for Kids website, www.dreamsforkids.org/father-wally-scholarship

6

Carrying On "Pup's" Legacy

Lord help me live from day to day, in such a humble sort of way, to give a smile, help lift a load, for those I meet along life's road, and when I come to my journey's end, my life I have not lived in vain, if one dear friend can smile and say "I'm glad I met him on life's way."

~ Author unknown

With Father Wally's blueprint blazing on my computer screen, I left a message on his voicemail. That afternoon, as I awaited his return call, I got a phone call from a young man named Jamal. He was one of the kids closest to Father Wally. Jamal told me that Father Wally had not answered his phone calls that entire day. He and some of the kids had gone to the parish and, uncharacteristically, Father Wally did not answer the bell to his room. The kids asked someone to check his room and he was found slumped over at his desk. It was March 8, 2001. Father Walter Brennan had died of a massive heart attack.

I was scheduled to have lunch with Father Wally the next

day. We had spoken just the day before, after he e-mailed his blueprint to me. That he was now gone was difficult for me to comprehend. When someone is taken away from us suddenly, we may have a difficult time processing the reality. Depending on the circumstances, we are often left with unfinished business and an unshakable sense of regret.

However, as I slowly came to terms with this sudden, harsh reality, I was filled with a sense of peace that a great man had completed his work among us, and was now safe at home. Father Wally's life was complete and because of the way he had lived, and how deeply he connected to us, he will always be with us.

To me, he was the finest example of someone who walks his talk. He was the people's priest. Father Walter Brennan took his faith and his obligations directly to the people. Finishing the brilliant blueprint of his life's work was one of the final, and possibly the very last act of his life. What a blessing it was that Father Wally completed his manuscript and left it as a guide for us to move forward and to continue his work.

The memorial wake for Father Wally lasted all through-out the day as he lay in state within the Basilica of Our Lady of Sorrows. Father Wally's funeral mass was scheduled for 7 p.m. that same evening. During the day, Jack Brennan, Wally's brother, had encountered a man at the wake who was crying in a distant row. Jack walked back to see him and asked, "Did you know Father Wally?" The man looked up and said, "Know him? He raised me."

Footprints in the Sand

At the deepest level, it's real love and care that people crave. Give those things, and you'll receive them. Through your caring deeds and actions, you'll truly make your mark on the world.

~ Howard Martin

The breadth and depth of the people Father Walter Brennan had touched was magnificent to behold. In all, over a thousand people came to pay their respects to Father Wally. People came from DePaul University, the academic community, students from as far back as the 1960's, parents of students, Chicago area politicians and leaders, and perhaps most importantly, people from the Lawndale and Westside communities of Chicago. The cross-section of those in attendance for the funeral mass was astounding. Together, students who had become lawyers and judges, business executives and entrepreneurs, sat with people who had grown up in a neighborhood isolated by poverty.

People, now middle-aged and secure, whom Father Wally had driven to school as children because there was no one else to drive them, and those for whom he had bought textbooks or clothes or food, attended the funeral. Ex-prisoners, whom he had counseled, attended as well. He visited prisons and jails often and counseled and cared for those who were incarcerated.

Countless adults, whom Father Wally "raised," brought their children to pay their respects to the man whose legacy continues to live in them.

Father Wally always had a group of kids with whom he maintained the strongest ties and there, in the middle of the church, center row, that entire group of kids tearfully huddled. Among this group were those kids who had found him when he did not answer the bell days before.

I was honored to be asked to deliver Father Wally's eulogy. In my words to the congregation of Father Wally's living legacy,

I drew from his blueprint, discussing how it represented his philosophy and approach to bridging the gap between various cultures. The diversity of those in attendance was a strong and powerful testament to his wisdom. The life of Father Wally had not just brought us together for a day, but instead, had connected us for a lifetime. He had filled our minds with knowledge and filled our hearts with compassion.

One of those present at the funeral was a man named Dale Tobias, who has become a trusted friend. A few days earlier, I had searched for Dale at the Ray Meyer Center basketball court to tell him the sad news. He was from the neighborhood. Father Wally had encouraged him in his studies, and became a constant presence in his life as he attended DePaul University. Dale attended, graduated law school, became a noteworthy attorney, and now works for the Chicago Transit Authority. He told me that he was at a complete loss. He said that he had spoken to Father Wally every day.

I asked Dale if he had spoken to him recently and he replied, "I spoke with Father Wally every single day for the past twenty-five years. I can tell you every place he has been and I spoke to him there. Italy, Ireland, Minnesota...every single day we spoke, no matter what."

Father Wally had also perfected the lost art of letter writing. He always sent handwritten notes to us all, never missing an anniversary, birthday, holiday or special occasion. So profound was their personal effect, that Dale had kept every single letter and card that Father Wally had ever sent to him.

Father Wally had taken Dale under his wing and encouraged him to believe in his dreams and convinced him that, no matter what the odds, Dale could achieve those dreams. He told Dale that he could count on him always being there for him and that he would never give up on him. It was twenty-five years later and still Father Wally had kept his word to him, as he had done for so many others.

In his ministry, Father Wally helped countless kids attend

and graduate from college, but more importantly, he drew no distinction between white or blue collar. If you aspired to work in the trades or to repair cars, he would help you get there and would inspire you to be the best.

Father Wally understood the importance of recruiting and mentoring kids who were at great risk, yet he also made it a habit to single out those who had the best chance of making a profound and lasting difference. Those were the kids who received the jobs around the church, were able to spend the most time with him, and were the ones with whom he maintained the closest ties. In a neighborhood filled with poverty and despair, Father Wally became an outpost of hope and the training ground for a life of promise.

The kids in Father Wally's inner circle were chosen for their willingness to learn how to make a difference, not just in their own lives, but also in the lives of those children who would follow them. The refuge of the rectory and the time spent with Father Wally would not only save them from negative influences in the neighborhood, but would also give them the skills to be future role models. His enduring lesson was a different look at the law of Karma: "That which is given to you, you give back tenfold."

For Those Who Love there are no Goodbyes

I asked God to take away my pain. God said, "No."
It is not for me to take away, but for you to give it up.

I asked God to make my handicapped child whole.
God said, "No."
Her spirit was whole, her body was only temporary.

I asked God to grant me patience. God said, "No."
Patience is a by-product of tribulations; it isn't
granted, it is earned.

I asked God to give me happiness. God said, "No."
I give you blessings. Happiness is up to you.

I asked God to spare me pain. God said, "No."
Suffering draws you apart from worldly cares and
brings you closer to me.

I asked God to make my spirit grow. God said, "No."
You must grow on your own, but I will prune you to
make you fruitful.

I asked God for all things that I might enjoy life. God
said, "No."
I will give you life so that you may enjoy all things.

I asked God to help me love others, as much as he
loves me. God said...

"Ahhhh, finally you have the idea."

~ Author Unknown

I had met all of the kids over the years. They had their own name for Father Wally: "Pup." It was short for "Puppy Dog," one of the numerous street names Father Wally would come up with to call the kids.

The sudden loss of Father Wally was devastating to the kids in his inner circle. They were the ones who saw him every day. They were the ones who found him when he didn't answer his bell. I saw the pain on their faces as I looked out over the church. He was so close to those kids and he meant so much to them. How could they carry on? What would become of them?

Having walked over to where the kids were sitting in the church to say hello and to share our grief, I learned their loss was crushing. Father Wally was only sixty-five-years old at the time of his death, not old by contemporary standards but there seemed to be so many years left for him to be with us.

I handed one of my business cards to each of the kids and wrote my cell phone number, telling them that we all had to stick together now, even more than before. We would have to carry on together in Pup's spirit. To stay connected would further his legacy and would reaffirm all that he had taught us. I encouraged each of the kids to call me at any time, for any reason.

"Let's keep his work going. Let's keep our connection strong. The greatest gift he gave us," I told them, "was bringing us all together. The greatest gift we can give back is to stay together and pass on his work."

One of those young men, Devon Coleman, called me the very next morning. He said to me, "I'm really sorry for calling you so soon." I reminded Devon that I had asked him to give me a call for anything, at anytime. He was calling from his car and had become distraught while driving to meet Pup for lunch, as he did nearly every day. He did not realize until he pulled into the church parking lot that Pup was no longer there. Devon had been on autopilot.

The loss of Father Wally was so profound that in the days that followed, it seemed inconceivable that it had occurred at all. The other kids in the church that day, Jamal, Quintel, Rashon, and Kiarri all had similar experiences to share in the days following Father Wally's funeral. I am fortunate to have been granted their trust and to have developed a mentor relationship with each of the young men. We are still in regular contact and continue to share Father Wally's dream.

Within several weeks, the remaining kids joined us, along with Dale, to create the Father Wally Program, which is now a permanent part of Dreams for Kids' programming. Our mission is simply to carry on his work. To develop the program, we enrolled Father Wally's extended family, the many students he had impacted at DePaul University over the years, the members of my fraternity, and the core group of individuals with whom Father Wally made a profound difference.

Together, we have embraced the blueprint of Father Wally's life and are doing what we can to help sustain this great man's legacy. In following Father Wally's lead, we are humbled by the far-reaching impact of his life's work, and it inspires us to help all those we can in his name.

The Living Legacy

One person can make a difference and every person should try.

~ John Fitzgerald Kennedy

The Father Wally Program is an outreach scholarship program designed to aid worthy students from the neighborhood to continue with their education. The program also serves as an emotional outlet for those who want to keep Father Wally's spirit alive and to keep the core group of Father Wally's beneficiaries connected. This program and its mission have become an important part of Dreams for Kids.

The five young men of Father Wally's final inner circle were all attending college when he passed on. Father Wally had known each of them for most of their lives. Not only had they lost their most avid supporter, but their college careers were in jeopardy. They needed financial support to make it through. At Dreams for Kids, in the spirit of the newly created Father Wally Program, we took the attitude that no matter what it takes, we were going to make sure that those kids had the opportunity to finish their university education. The Father Wally Program, and the funds we raised in our mentor's name, has accomplished that goal.

After Jamal finished college, he went on to earn two advanced degrees, a Masters in Finance and a Masters in Business Administration. Jamal has also recently passed the CPA exam. Devon is currently the owner of a landscaping business and is the managing member of a real estate investment company. His company rehabilitates properties in distressed neighborhoods. Kiarri finished college and obtained a Masters Degree in Business Administration and is working full-time in Atlanta. Quintel completed his studies at Southern Illinois University.

Most importantly, all four young men respond on a moment's notice to assist Dreams for Kids and its mission. They are fixtures at our annual Holiday Party for the kids and Jamal even fills in as Santa Claus. He said we needed a "Brother Claus" anyway, so it might as well be him!

The core principle of our ongoing Father Wally Program is that it must extend beyond the awarding of scholarship funds and also must focus on giving back to the next generation. We require our recipients to accept the responsibility of doing well in school, securing a meaningful career and keeping the program sustained for others. In doing so, we are keeping alive the legacy and spirit of a great man, whose words continue to resonate in our lives: "Remember that which is given to you, you give back tenfold."

Today, when you drive down the streets of the Westside and Lawndale communities of Chicago, homes are being refurbished and businesses are returning to the neighborhood. When you see the look of hope on the faces of the residents, you remember a time not long ago. If you close your eyes, you can see a little Irish priest they called Pup, dressed in shorts and gym shoes, wearing a Cubs' hat and walking the streets of a forgotten community, late at night, in a neighborhood that is now full of Brennans.

Long before the rebirth of the Westside, as Father Wally was walking its streets to deliver hope, there was another neighborhood in Chicago whose residents lived in equal desperation. In that neighborhood, Englewood, there lived a woman who was also small in stature. As with Father Wally, it would take a walk down the dangerous streets of her neighborhood to awaken a lifelong passion to make a difference. She too became larger than life. Dreams for Kids walked side by side with this remarkable woman and found the highway to a Christmas dream.

7

Clara's Way is the High Way

Life is fleeting. But if you live your life in hope, hope that you can make a difference somehow, and you strive to succeed, then your life will last forever and you will never be forgotten.

~ Samuel Johnson Adams

In 1987, Clara Kirk, as co-founder of the West Englewood United Organization (WEUO), was an active community volunteer on Chicago's Southside. WEUO was founded in 1983 to act as an advocate for the members of the community who were having difficulty paying their mortgages and utilities.

Once known as Junction Grove and recognized as one of the great rail and commerce crossroads in the United States, Englewood was a neighborhood that had fallen on very hard times in the 1970's. The closing of the rail lines and stockyards brought a wave of business and plant closings and caused a massive loss of jobs resulting in the majority of the residents living below the poverty level. Historic homes built after the Great

Chicago Fire began to decay and were left abandoned.

One night Clara received a phone call from another member of WEUO. Clara's friend insisted that she meet members of the organization right away at a location a few blocks away.

Upon arriving at the address, Clara asked her friends why they had asked her to come to this boarded-up, abandoned building. "Because you have to come inside and see for yourself," her friends replied. Clara remembers thinking that there was no way she was going to walk into that scary looking building, when, just then, its makeshift door opened and a small child stood in the doorway.

"A little girl, no more than six-years-old, with a pretty little dress on, looked at me and I felt the presence of a beautiful angel," Clara recalled.

"I Live Here..."

"I thought that if this little girl can come out of this terrible building then I am surely going to go in. I asked the girl why she was in that building." Clara continued in a quiet voice, "I will never forget the sad way she looked at me when she answered, 'I live here.'"

As Clara walked into the building, what she saw changed her life forever. Inside this abandoned building, with no heat, electricity or running water, were at least six families, living in conditions that brought her to tears. Even today, more than twenty years later, Clara cannot talk about what she saw that night without being overcome with emotion.

"There were mothers and seniors and little babies and grown men. All of them living in a place filled with water, garbage and rats. I thought, this is my neighborhood and this is how these people have to live. This is how they have to survive."

Clara Kirk had made a commitment that night, in the sadness of that building; she would find a way to help the people in

Englewood find a more humane way to live.

The next day, in a style that many have grown to know and admire, Clara picked up the phone and called the Mayor of Chicago. "I told the people at the Mayor's Office that the Mayor had to know how people were living in his city, in conditions no better than those of a third world country."

That day, Mayor Harold Washington responded by finding shelter for all of the people in that building, and by requesting a meeting with Clara Kirk.

Clara's House

Sometimes our light goes out but is blown into flame by another human being. Each of us owes our deepest thanks to those who have rekindled this light.

~ Albert Schweitzer

Clara was no stranger to helping others. Small in stature but with the heart of a giant, she was a 4'11" grandmother of twelve, who had spent eighteen years of her life opening the doors to her home and adopting children in need, even as she raised her own five children. Clara Kirk became Englewood's foster parent. Her daughter Sabrina told me recently that she could never remember a time while growing up when the kids Clara took into their home did not outnumber her own brothers and sisters.

When asked about her life's work, Clara told the Chicago Sun-Times, "It's the kids that I want to take care of; they don't ask to be born."

In the mid-1980's, Clara and the members of the WEUO had persuaded Catholic Charities to donate a rectory, which had been closed and was next to a grade school. It was WEUO's hope that their organization could somehow raise the money needed to rehabilitate the building and open a community center so that people could come for a meal and stay warm during the cold nights.

Now that Clara had brought to light the plight of the homeless in Chicago, Mayor Washington had other ideas. The Mayor wanted her to open a shelter for victims of domestic violence and for homeless women and their children. The Mayor asked Clara to raise the money needed to reopen the rectory building and told her that he would help her do it.

Clara Kirk and the members of WEUO began an effort that resulted in history being made in the City of Chicago.

On February 27, 1987, after a tireless effort to raise enough funds to supplement the financial assistance of the city, Clara's House opened its doors to the homeless, abused, and lost women and children of Englewood. The facility became the model for shelters across the country and would someday bring Clara Kirk to a *House* of an entirely different kind in Washington D.C.

A Shelter of Hope

One does not have to be an angel in order to be saint.
~ Albert Schweitzer

It was never Clara Kirk's intention to merely find shelter for the homeless and abandoned of Englewood. She wanted those who had lost their way to find their future. In fact, Clara insisted on it.

"When someone is poor or when they have been abused or when they have lost everything, they need help, but more than anything, they have to help themselves. I will not beg, borrow and give my life for anyone who does not help themselves," Clara strongly declared.

That is why there are rules posted on the bulletin board for all to see at Clara's House. There are no exceptions to those rules. They apply to every resident and they are applied as soon as each person walks in the front door of an immaculately clean and orderly home.

As soon as the front door opens, visitors and residents alike realize that Clara's House is no ordinary shelter. In fact, as soon as you become aware of Clara's three times a day, top to bottom, cleaning schedule, immaculate bunk beds in spotless bedrooms and the dining room table set for one of three nutritious meals, you realize immediately that this place is a shelter in name only. Clara's House is truly a home and a safe haven of hope.

Clara's House is a sixty-nine bed facility, and the beds are solidly and attractively constructed bunk beds dressed with clean linens. The beds are located on the second floor of the facility, in rooms separated for families and individuals.

The mission of Clara's House is to provide emergency transitional housing and to stabilize and preserve the family structure.

With the purpose of assisting the residents in regaining independent living, it provides the residents with medical attention, health screenings, food, clothing, educational and job training, and holistic counseling. However, in Clara's House the old adage is most definitely followed: "To whom much is given, much is expected."

The living room, kitchen and dining room are on the first floor of Clara's House, and posted on the bulletin board for all to see are the Resident Rules. Mandatory rules, such as:

- No sleeping between the hours of 7:00 a.m. and 7:00 p.m.
- No alcohol
- No drugs
- Attendance at all Parenting Classes, Health Care Screenings, Family Counseling, and Drug and Alcohol Awareness Classes is mandatory

In total, there are twenty-four rules, simply stated but rigorously enforced. Although I knew the answer quite well, I once asked Clara, as she gave a group of visitors a tour of the house, what she would do if a resident came back to the house at 9:05 p.m., five minutes after the mandatory curfew. She replied with a hard and fast look, "I would tell them to pack their bags and leave."

Clara makes it clear that she believes that in order for someone to reclaim their life, they must be disciplined and must follow rules. She will give every waking minute of her day to help others. But if those whom she attempts to help do not respect themselves and show respect to others, and if they do not strive every day to improve their lives and to also help others, then Clara Kirk simply has no time for them.

For 120 days, Clara's House provides the groundwork for building a foundation for future stability and for a return to independent living. Seventy-percent of what every resident earns during their stay through employment or through Public Aid is given to Clara's House.

The entire amount is returned to the resident at the end of their stay so that they will have enough money for a security deposit on an apartment of their own and for their basic needs. At the end of their stay at Clara's House, Clara's system would have provided the opportunity to be prepared to begin the rest of their lives.

However, Clara found that for women with children, 120 days simply was not enough time to ensure that the family structure was secure, and that the children had a stable environment. She sensed a crisis and the eventual return to sheltered living or worse.

To Thrive, Not Just Survive

Every step you take, is a step away from where you used to be.

~ Brian Chargualaf

With an eye to the future security and prosperity of those to whom she had given shelter, Clara expanded her vision.

In 1992, while serving on the Board of Directors of the WEUO, I received a phone call from Clara. I picked up the phone and before I could say hello, Clara said, "Get over here right now!" I had known her for three years and I knew not to ask why. You simply do not ask Clara Kirk why, and you certainly do not waste any time in responding to her request.

Thirty minutes after I hung up the phone, I was standing on 63rd Street looking at a large three story, boarded-up, abandoned building sitting on a huge corner lot. Before the economic downturn and rail closings of the early 1970's, 63rd Street was a district so vital that it was recognized as the City of Chicago's largest and most lucrative retail shopping district, second only to Chicago's Loop district. In 1991, once proud 63rd Street was so desolate, that the few buildings still standing, among vast empty lots, were only a court order away from demolition.

"That's our building. That's Second Stage," declared Clara with proud conviction. "Do we own it?" I asked. "Of course not, that is why you are going to find a way to get it!" she exclaimed.

So began a six-year journey that led us through the frustrations of Housing Court, and the daunting task of raising over $1.5 million in private, city, state and federal funds to fully rehabilitate, within stringent city codes, a completely gutted building.

On May 15th 1998, against all legal, economic and political odds, Clara's Second Stage Housing opened. Today the facility provides a total of thirteen furnished apartments for which residents pay an average rent of $200 per month. The residents are single mothers in need of more than just temporary shelter.

Clara's Second Stage Housing adopts all of her mandatory health, work, and parental training. The mission is to give women an opportunity to build a secure future and to provide limitless opportunities for their children.

In 2003, recognizing the importance of parental influence on the academic achievement of their children, Clara Kirk established Clara's House Academic Center, which provides GED classes for adults, after school tutoring for children, as well as computer training for both children and adults.

From Clara's House to the White House

If something comes to life in others because of you, then you have made an approach to immortality.
~ Norman Cousins

Since taking her private crusade to help children on to the very streets of Englewood to stare down homelessness and challenge those who have the means to do something about it, Clara Kirk has provided over 10,000 women and children refuge. She has given them the opportunity to build a foundation for the rest of their lives as well as for the generations to come.

In 1972, Jacqueline Kennedy Onassis, U.S. Senator Robert Taft, Jr. and Sam Beard founded the American Institute for Public Service, to create a Nobel Prize for public and community service, and named it, The Jefferson Awards. The Jefferson Awards, established in the spirit of Thomas Jefferson's idea that "life, liberty and the pursuit of happiness are our national rights," is presented on two levels: national and local. National award recipients represent a "Who's Who" of outstanding Americans. On the local level, Jefferson Awards' recipients are ordinary people who do extraordinary things without expectation of recognition or reward.

In April of 1996, Clara Kirk was recognized as one of those who have done the extraordinary and was awarded the Jefferson Award for the State of Illinois.

Later that same year, Clara became one of only 100 individuals ever to have been awarded the National Jefferson Award for lifetime achievement and contributions to her community and was recognized in a ceremony in Washington D.C., as an enduring example that, "One person can make a difference."

In 1997, 20,000 nominees of outstanding Americans were submitted to the prestigious Jefferson Awards' Committee, chaired by Presidents Bill Clinton, George H.W. Bush, Jimmy Carter, and Gerald Ford. From that great list of humanitarians, Clara Kirk was chosen as one of "America's 25 Unsung Heroes" and was recognized as, one of our "great Americans…. with a legacy of community service that will last for generations." On that special night Clara Kirk was inducted into the Jefferson Awards Hall of Fame.

The following year, in 1998, President Bill Clinton invited Clara Kirk to the White House and presented her with the prestigious President's Award in recognition of her life's work.

The American Dream

Today Clara Kirk works in a tiny office on the first floor of Clara's Second Stage Housing and hears the unusual and long forgotten sound of construction. Outside Clara's front door, historic 63rd Street is being revitalized as the cornerstone of a $525 million City of Chicago redevelopment plan for Englewood.

Homes throughout this still very poor community are slowly being rehabilitated. Rising property values have Clara worried that her long-suffering neighbors and friends will not be able to afford to stay in the community that they had never given up on. "We must have a Third Stage. People must be able to own their own home," Clara strongly stated.

In her office, in 2005, Clara received a call from Mayor Richard M. Daley. The Mayor asked Clara to come to City Hall right away. When she arrived she was taken to a meeting in Mayor Daley's office, which was attended by several city Commissioners as well as by a prominent local builder.

When Clara walked in, Mayor Daley stood and hugged her and told her that the City of Chicago had acquired numerous vacant lots on two city blocks in Englewood and would begin construction of a large community of homes. The homes would be built for the residents of Englewood to provide permanent housing for poor, homeless, and abused women and children. The community would be named Clara's Village.

I will always remember the phone call I received from Clara that day. She was in the lobby of City Hall. She had gone out of the exit doors on each of the four sides of City Hall and had come back in. She could not get her bearings in a building she had been in countless times. "I am trying to believe what just happened. Is it true?" Clara asked. It was true. It was now almost twenty years later, after a long proud journey, filled with tears and an unbreakable spirit that began with her phone call to the Mayor. Now the Mayor had called Clara. All the stages of her life's work had been achieved. All of Clara's improbable dreams had come true.

Today, in Clara's Village, located in the heart of Englewood, the sounds of joyful children can be heard, playing and laughing in a beautiful, safe and secure community. If you listen closely, within those sounds of happy children can be heard the voice of a beautiful little angel. You can hear her say, "I live here!"

8

Here Comes Santa Claus

One hundred years from now it will not matter what
kind of car you drove, what kind of house you lived in,
how much you had in your bank account, or what your
clothes looked like. But the world may be a little better
because you were important in the life of a child.

~ Anonymous

When Clara Kirk was at the beginning of her history making journey, I had just graduated from law school and had begun my career as an attorney. After a few years, I began to listen to that voice inside of me that was a constant reminder of where I had come from and of how fortunate I now was in my life.

In 1989, my mother attended an event where I was being recognized by an organization that I had assisted. Also in attendance were many of my friends. It was there that my mother took me aside. Rather than dwell on some award, my mom did what she did best; she reminded me of how much more I could do.

My mother reminded me that to have so many friends and

for them to be from various backgrounds was a blessing and an opportunity. The people in that room had actually come into my life, in part, because of a lesson my mother had taught me long before. It was my mother's advice to always seek friends who were older than me and also younger than me, and to be especially open to those who were from all walks of life.

So, in the midst of those diverse friends who now graced my life, my mother made the observation that it would be great if I could bring my friends together for a common purpose and do something that would be worthwhile, and would make a lasting difference for kids who were in need.

On that evening, Dreams for Kids was born.

The Beginning of a Dream

> *The joy of brightening other's lives, bearing each other's burdens, easing other's loads, and supplanting empty hearts and lives with generous gifts, becomes for us the magic of Christmas.*
>
> ~ W.C. Jones

In one of those moments that assure you that things happen in our world as they should, when I awoke the next morning the name Dreams for Kids immediately came to my mind.

As I contacted each of my friends, who became the first Board of Directors of Dreams for Kids, there was great enthusiasm behind the idea and for the creation of the organization. The only thing missing was that we had absolutely no idea what we were going to do. What we never could have known was that the future had much more in store for us than we could have ever imagined.

One of the very first people to whom I spoke about Dreams for Kids was a friend who worked as the secretary for one of our Board members, then Sheriff of Cook County. It seems that a woman had just been in to see the Sheriff to ask for his support for a shelter she had built in Englewood. My friend gave me a telephone number and I was soon speaking with Clara Kirk.

It did not take long to discover that Clara was no ordinary woman and that she had no time for formalities, and definitely had no patience for a long courtship. When she answered the phone, I introduced myself and I asked her if there might be some way Dreams for Kids could help the kids living in the shelter. Clara immediately answered, "If you want to know about the shelter and provide assistance, then you need to make a visit." I asked, "When would be a good time?" She answered, "Right now. If you are serious, you will come right now."

When I hung up the phone, the next call I made was to Bill Nolan, an officer with the Fraternal Order of Police. He was one of the first of my friends to agree on a moment's notice to join our Board of Directors, served as our first Vice-President. Bill said he would be right over to pick me up, and twenty minutes later we were on our way to Englewood to meet Clara Kirk.

When Clara opened the front door of Clara's House, she immediately took us on a tour of the immaculate facility and explained the guidelines and strict rules of the shelter. She said we were welcome to help in any way we could, but that we should remember that the kids who were living in this house had lost everything and what they really needed was hope.

As we drove back to our offices, Bill and I knew we had to do something for those kids. We felt an immediate connection to Clara and held a deep admiration for what she was doing in a neighborhood that was so unbelievably desolate. We could not imagine what the holidays could be like for the kids who lived in any shelter. We decided right then and there, in Bill's car, that Dreams for Kids would come to Clara's House and would bring the Christmas spirit with it.

The next day I called Clara and asked her if she would like us to host a Christmas Party for the Shelter. Without hesitation, Clara said, "What day are you going to have it?" In what became the first of many long-standing traditions, we chose the Saturday before Christmas, which happened to fall on Christmas Eve that year.

Several days before our party, Clara called to give us the names of the fifty-four children who were currently living at the shelter. She warned, "If you are bringing gifts, you better bring extra, because we might take in more kids the night before."

Our entire Board of Directors went shopping. We made sure we had gifts for each of the kids and food for a complete Christmas dinner for everyone at Clara's House. We recruited our own Santa Claus and awoke early Saturday morning to vehicles packed with gifts and food.

The Tradition Begins

Twas the night before Christmas, when all through the house, not a creature was stirring-not even a mouse. The stockings were hung by the chimney with care, in hopes that St. Nicholas soon would be there.

~ Clement C. Moore

Prior to arriving at Clara's House, our group established another tradition and met for breakfast. My mother was in attendance as was my brother Jim, my sister Kathleen and my niece, Heather. In total, there were twenty of us that December morning in 1989. At that first breakfast, we all began to feel the spirit of the day, and as it would become apparent, the true spirit of Christmas. After we broke bread, the caravan of vehicles, with toys stacked inside from window to window, headed for Englewood.

We pulled up in front of the shelter and while the kids were still sleeping, quietly unloaded all of the food and gifts. We set up a food table and carefully arranged gifts under the shelter's tiny Christmas tree.

In 1989, my niece Heather was just an eight-month-old infant, fastened in a child carrier and resting on the couch. Twenty years later, Heather drove to the Christmas party that she has attended her entire life. The Dreams for Kids' Christmas Party is part of her life, has helped shape her character, and will, I am certain, continue to be a special part of her life far into the future. Heather has the greatest enthusiasm each year for this party. For her, this is Christmas. She knows this as tradition, as the true spirit of the season, and she would not have it any other way.

On December 24th 1989, on the first floor of Clara's House, we could hear children stirring upstairs. We could only imagine the excitement as the kids began to experience the magic of Christmas. All fifty-four kids were now scrambling to find a seat at the top of the stairs. All that childhood wonder was bottled up inside of them. *Does Santa really exist? Did Santa really come? Did Santa bring me a gift? Are there cookies?*

We quickly devised a sequence of events. Santa would arrive after the kids had come downstairs. Our recruited Santa, actually an off-duty Chicago police officer, would wait outside holding a bag of smaller gifts. This was my mother's suggestion. Englewood, however, as Clara told us, was not a place where you'd want to linger outside for too long, particularly with a bag of gifts.

Santa waited at the corner of the building, just to the side of the front windows. We hadn't figured how we would summon him at the right moment. As this was happening for the first time, it may not have occurred to us that we were creating one of many long-standing traditions.

What If There Was No Christmas?

Here comes Santa Claus! Here comes Santa Claus!
Right down Santa Claus Lane! Bells are ringing,
children singing; All is merry and bright.

Inside the shelter, Clara summoned the kids downstairs, and for anyone who has had the privilege of witnessing children literally flying down the stairs on Christmas morning, imagine those kids who have awakened early on this special day in a strange bed, being sheltered from the streets. I am not sure if their little feet even touched the stairs.

As we stood surrounded by a room full of happy kids, someone asked if the kids thought Santa was coming. After bringing the excitement up a notch, we quickly realized we didn't have a plan to actually get the word to Santa. He was outside, oblivious to the hysteria inside the house.

Someone said to the kids, "I don't think Santa knows you're here. Maybe if you sing a song, he'll hear you and stop by. Why don't we all sing *Jingle Bells?*" Thus began the happiest of our traditions. Fifty-four children started singing *Jingle Bells* with all the enthusiasm and volume imaginable. With each stanza, the singing grew louder and louder. As soon as the words hit the street, Santa knew that it was time.

As Santa turned to walk from the corner of the building to the main entrance, he passed under the windows. You could only see the top of his red Santa hat from inside the shelter, but the moment couldn't have been choreographed any better. As soon as the kids saw that famous red hat moving across the house, they all rushed to the windows and piled on top of each other for a better look.

Seconds later, Santa burst through the door and let out a hearty "Ho, Ho, Ho!" In a moment frozen in time, it was Frank Capra and Norman Rockwell all wrapped up in one. As all the kids, wrapped in complete happiness and joy, mobbed Santa in his bright red suit and bag of overflowing gifts, I realized that we had brought what Clara had asked for, the greatest gift of all—Hope.

I will always remember looking back to the side of the room. Seated in chairs against the wall were all the mothers, including my own. They were all smiling.

After Santa sat down in his chair, each child sat on his lap for as long as they wished, and on my mother's insistence, Santa gave each mother gloves and perfume. Soon after all the gifts had been opened, and the kids were busy playing with the many toys scattered on the floor, we prepared to leave so that the residents could enjoy their meal and the rest of a special day.

As we headed for the front door, Clara thanked each of us. As I gave Clara a hug, I told her the Christmas party was the least we could do and it was special for all of us as well. Clara looked me in the eye and sternly said, "You don't understand, do you? If you had not come today, they would never even have known it was Christmas."

Twenty years later, the weight of that statement still hangs heavy on my heart and brings me to the exact moment and place in that shelter. Seeing the look on my face, Clara calmly explained that without this celebration she could not have even told the kids it was Christmas. It would have been better to let the day come and go without letting them know. There was no way the shelter could afford to buy gifts, and it would have been better to not disappoint them. They had so little to look forward to on such a special morning, after waking up in a strange bed, with no home of their own.

We left with the realization that we had provided Christmas cheer and hope for children whom would have never known the difference. In the quiet of the ride home, each of us realized that this was truly the essence and spirit of Christmas. Now twenty years later, for my niece and sister, for members of our Board and for me personally, Christmas with Clara *is* Christmas. I know I could not spend it any other way.

9

"Our Kids Will Talk About This For Years"

Whatever else be lost among the years, let us keep Christmas still a shining thing: Whatever doubts assail us, or what fears, let us hold close one day, remembering Its poignant meaning over the hearts of men. Let us get back our childhood faith again.

~ Grace Noll Crowell

What started as a single day of giving to those who had no home for Christmas, has grown into a tradition with a life of its own.

For many years, we continued to visit Clara's House on the Saturday before Christmas. After a couple of years, we added a new shelter to our schedule. When it became apparent there were so many kids who had so little, we created a single, huge Christmas party and hosted it at one location. Clara was sad to see the party move from her house, but understood the need to reach more kids. Since that time, she has traveled with her kids to every single party.

Our first location was Our Lady of Sorrows, the parish house of our spiritual advisor, Father Wally Brennan.

Eventually, the celebration outgrew that facility and we moved to Excalibur, an entertainment center near downtown Chicago. We held the celebration there for several more years until the need again outgrew the space.

Today, the Dreams for Kids' Annual Christmas Party is the largest of its kind for homeless and underprivileged children in Illinois. Each year, more than 1,200 children from all over Illinois, together with their parents, teachers, and social workers enter a Winter Wonderland for a truly spectacular day of fun and Christmas spirit.

Giving and Receiving

Joy increases as you give it, and diminishes as you try to keep it for yourself. In giving it, you will accumulate a deposit of joy greater than you ever believed possible.
~ Norman Vincent Peale

Each year, we choose a facility that provides interactive games and exhibits such as those found at our 2005 host facility, the nationally acclaimed Health World Children's Museum in Barrington, Illinois. With the generous sponsorship of Allstate Insurance Company, we arrange for transportation for children with disabilities and for those who are living in poverty.

As the kids step into a Christmas Dream, they walk past an honor guard of United States Marines, while being serenaded with carols by local church and high school choirs.

Every single child in attendance has his own name badge so that volunteers can address each child personally. Our Christmas Party would not be complete without clowns, jugglers, face-painters, and craft making, a tradition that was created twelve years ago by my sister Kathleen. The craft tables have become our party's prime attraction, with tables of kids, hundreds of them, concentrating hard at making that one special ornament to give to Mom. J.J. O'Connor's mother, Blanche, and her five daughters have now joined Kathleen as craft coordinators, and volunteers clamor to get a spot at one of the tables. Blanche personally recruits a group to bake, in her kitchen, over 1,200 gingerbread cookies prior to the party!

Of course, after a full lunch, the party is topped off with that special appearance by Santa Claus. We actually have four Santas now, in separate areas of the facilities—but we don't tell the kids. Yes, when Santa arrives, it is to the sound of more than a thousand kids singing *Jingle Bells*.

Every child now receives a shopping bag full of gifts, which are, in part, donated by the community, the U.S. Marines, and other social and civic groups. The International Brotherhood of Electrical Workers, Local #134, stores all 3,000 gifts prior to the party, and hosts a wrapping party two days before the event. The fundraising events and the gift drives, of course, start months in advance. The event is so popular that volunteers wanting to participate in the actual party must sign up on a waiting list.

Understanding the popularity of the party has not been difficult. The effect the party has on the kids is evident, but not to be lost is the effect of the party on the volunteers. Many volunteers come for the first time, in much the same state of mind that we were in sixteen years ago. They are there to make a contribution and to give during the *Season*. Little did we all know just how much we would receive in return.

Dreams for Kids receives so many letters to remind us of the impact of that special day, and even more experiences will forever live in the memory of all who have been touched by this day. I could fill the pages of this book with stories that would move you to tears and others that would make you laugh with joy. In twenty years, there are so many memories and snapshots of human nature that will last a lifetime.

I will never forget watching a little boy leave the basement of Our Lady of Sorrows Parish after Santa had left the building. This boy could not have been older than four or five-years-old, and he was dragging his shopping bag behind him with two hands; the bag nearly as tall as he was. When he got to the steps, he turned and saw me watching. He smiled and dragged the bag all the way back across the room and said to me, "This is the best gift I have ever gotten. Thank you so much for my truck. Merry Christmas." I watched him as he left and said a prayer, being reminded, once again, of the true spirit of Christmas.

I often think of the following story from several years ago, and when I do, I am reminded, once again, that the most deeply significant moments live in us as if they occurred only moments before. One of our volunteers, a woman in her sixties, was carrying one of the crafts. I said it was nice that she had the chance to make a craft for herself. As she looked at me, I could tell she was deeply moved, and she said she had not made it. Then she told me her Christmas story.

"A precious little girl, with beautiful braids in her hair had made this craft. I saw her walking around the party holding it in the palms of her two little hands. I told her, 'Your tree is beautiful!' She thanked me and said she worked very hard on it and really liked it. For the rest of the party I watched her as she carried it all around with pride. A few moments ago she was leaving with her mother and had searched to find me. This beautiful girl, who had no home to return to, said to me, 'Thank you so much for telling me that my tree was beautiful. I want you to have it.'"

Our volunteer let the tears fall as she held her tree and said, "I will never have an ornament that is more special to me. It will be the first ornament I put on my tree every year and I will treasure it." I stood and watched as our volunteer walked out the door, holding her tree in the palms of her two hands.

We received a letter from a first-time volunteer.

Dear Dreams for Kids,

I was raised in the Uptown area of Chicago's Northside and it was not a wonderful place. My parents never made a lot of money, but they loved and cared for my sisters and me. They sacrificed much of their lives to make our world a better place and our future a brighter opportunity. I owe much of my success in life to the example they set for me throughout their lives.

I volunteered for the Christmas Party and included my spouse, Carmel, and my two youngest children, Aaron (age 14) and Meghan (age 11). Their initial response to spending a whole day of their weekend during the holiday break was not favorable. I had to stress the importance of sharing life's bounty with others who have much less than us.

They needed to understand how great a gap exists between the rest of the world and ourselves. They could not appreciate it until they came into contact with it, experienced it to some small degree, and began to recognize the real need for each of us, in some small way, to make the world a better place for everyone.

It was an exhausting and exciting day. My whole family lost themselves in the children and their activities. They were so busy making sure the children enjoyed themselves that they were caught by surprise when the day came to an end. My special joy was seeing how much the children responded to my children. Aaron spent the entire day with a group of young people in wheelchairs. I asked one young girl if Aaron was doing a good job and she smiled and said that he was "very handsome." Meghan helped many children doing crafts and decorating cookies and she received so many hugs from the little ones.

When we were driving home afterwards, I asked the family how they felt about their day. Their response was wonderful. They wanted to sign up immediately for next year. Could they bring their friends? Are there any other events that help children? And then they started asking questions. Why this and why that? It was clear to me that their eyes had seen a different world where children worry more about their next meal and warm clothing than about video games and the latest fashion.

Ms. Kirk stated that the party opened the children's minds to a different world. Yes, that is true, especially for my children. Thanks again for allowing my family to share in this wonderful event.

David Ferst
Allstate Insurance Company

P.S. Is it possible to involve more young people in next year's event? I think the children attending the event make an immediate connection with young people that enhances their experience and memories of the event.

Mr. Ferst was referring to Clara Kirk and a conversation I had with her at that 2005 Christmas Party, which I shared with our volunteers after the party to thank them for making such an impact on the lives of so many kids.

At noon, as the party swirled around us, I found a quiet corner and had the pleasure of having lunch with my friend Clara, in the cafeteria of Health World Children's Museum, in the affluent suburb of Barrington, Illinois.

Clara looked out the window at the wide-open space and said, "Where we come from, the kids have never seen land like this. They have never even dreamed about a place like this. They wouldn't even think it was real. It's Disney World. Our kids don't go to Disney World. Bringing them here and treating them this way will change their lives."

I listened as Clara continued, "You see these kids will go back to school and talk about this day and tell all the other kids and their teachers. They will work harder in school and they will believe more in their future. You have shown them that this is all real and you have given them hope. They can believe it's possible to live like this. *Our kids will talk about this for years...*"

Dreams for Kids' work began in a small shelter, and each year the tradition of Christmas grew. However, Christmas is but one day and we knew the true spirit of giving could not be a one-time event. The first Christmas at Clara's House was the first day of the rest of Dreams for Kids' life. We had taken our first step; it was now time to walk.

10

Walking the Dream's Talk

Do not worry if you have built your castles in the air. They are where they should be. Now put foundations under them.

~ Henry David Thoreau

In Dreams for Kids' first seven years, with Jesse White, Father Wally and Clara Kirk leading the way, there were, unfortunately, never any shortages of children in need of assistance. There was Joshua, who was blinded by a stray bullet, Jeremy who lost his sight in an accident, and Nicole who needed a kidney transplant. A family on the Northside lost their home and everything they owned to a fire and there were clothes to buy for their five children.

It seemed every week there was more news of need. A high school graduate from the Westside had worked all summer, borrowed money from his sister and his mother and $200 from his grandmother, but was still $750 short of what he needed to begin his first year at college. He was the first in his family to ever attend college, and we made sure he did.

The students at Oscar Meyer School had the opportunity

to go to our nation's Capital, but the poorest of them would not be able to take the educational trip of their lifetime. A girl from the south suburbs had leukemia and her parents' medical insurance had run out. A father of four children on the Northside had lost his job and in another month would lose his family's house, and with it, their residency for school.

You never read about the plight of any of these kids or their families, and it was a reminder that these situations were all too commonplace. Responding to those situations and to many other people who might otherwise have been lost in silent desperation became our standard.

Sometimes the pain was close to home. One of my secretaries' young nieces was diagnosed with lymphoma, and her family struggled in ways one could only imagine. For Natalie Benda, we helped organize a benefit that would serve as a gathering place for family, friends and community to come together and remind Natalie and her family they were not alone.

One of my fraternity brothers lost his baby daughter when she failed to wake up one morning. Dreams for Kids established the Kelly Christine Raimondi Fund so that, each year, her grade school could award a family who had suffered hardship, the financial assistance to ensure their children could stay in school. The fund continues today, and Kelly's name and memory lives in others.

In 1993 my mother, who inspired it all, was diagnosed with breast cancer. We responded before it was too late for my mother to know how important her life was and how significant her contributions were, not just to all of her children, but to all of the children who Dreams for Kids has helped because of her.

We immediately endowed the Patricia Tuohy Scholarship Fund. My mother's brother, Jim Barrett, came in from Florida to announce the scholarship at our annual golf outing event. Together we went home that night and delivered the news to Mom. My Aunt Joan told me later that, throughout all of my mother's difficulties in life, she had never seen my mother cry—

until the night my mom called to tell my aunt about her scholarship. That night my mom let the tears flow, knowing that women who struggled as she did, would be helped in her name.

It has been twelve years since the night I had the opportunity to tell my mother how much she mattered to the world, and to remind her how much she meant to my own world. The passage of time has only reminded me more that the true blessing received that night was the realization that every day was a good day to tell my mother how much I loved her. The only special occasion needed was the gift of another day. I am so grateful for that blessing, and the peace it now gives me.

The same year that we announced the Patricia Tuohy Scholarship, and each year since my mother's passing, Dreams for Kids has found a woman, who is living day-to- day, giving all she has so her children can have a future. Each of these special mothers asks the same question: Why was I chosen? We tell her she has a *guardian angel*.

'The Tuition Angels'

> *A mother holds her children's hands for a while, their hearts forever.*
>
> ~ Author unknown

The first mother who was awarded the Patricia Tuohy Scholarship was Sue Linda Moore. Father Wally told us her story, and we quietly reached out to her daughter Jamie's high school.

Ms. Moore had raised her three children on her own. Her youngest daughter was in her final year of high school, was a straight A student, and was close to earning the credits for acceptance to college. Jamie's mom was struggling to find the tuition money so that she could remain in school. Shortly after my mother's passing, I received the following letter, which I have always kept close to me.

Dear Mr. Tuohy,

This letter has taken me so long to write. How do you just say thank you to someone who has changed your world?

I'm a mother, much like a lot of mothers, who adores her children. It has been difficult raising my son, and two daughters, but it has also been one of my greatest blessings and joys. Jamie is my youngest child, and she is such an exceptional child, never complaining about not having the many things she should have.

Writing these words brings tears to my eyes, because she really deserves so much. I'm so sincere about having Jamie finish school at I.H.M. and the school has been so good in understanding my roller coaster situation. I really had nowhere to turn and our backs were up against the wall. I had run out of resources and the school could do no more. If Jamie were removed from the school she would have to transfer to one that was dangerous and she would leave all those she knew. She would maybe never have the opportunity to go to college.

We were really backed against the wall with no way out when the tuition angels went to work.

When Jamie told me what you had done, I had to pull over and stop the car. I'm so emotional lately. No one loves one child more than another and I wanted so much for Jamie.

Anyway, it just doesn't seem like enough, but thank you so much. I hope I raised my children in the same way your mother raised you and all my love and effort is helping to produce a human being with the love and compassion you exhibit. God bless you and your loved ones.

Ms. Sue Linda Arrington Moore

The Patricia Tuohy Scholarship award allowed Jamie to finish her final year and she went on to graduate from college.

Today, when I want to imagine what a *tuition angel* really looks like, I close my eyes and I see my mom.

Grateful Stewards

More than ever, and with good reason, people are concerned about the destination of their generosity. If someone is making a financial contribution to a cause that has touched their heart, they want to know that the intent of their gift is being fulfilled. *Where is the money really going?*

With increasing stories of misuse and misapplication of donor funds to charitable causes around the world, it can be very discouraging for people. In 1989, Dreams for Kids made a pledge and incorporated that pledge into our initial, non-profit, corporate bi-laws, as well as into our mission. We would be accountable to those who financially supported the kids whom we represented.

For our entire existence, our administration and operating expense to program expense ratio has been one of the very lowest in the country, at over 90%. In 2008, it was 94%. This simply means that, in 2008, for every dollar contributed by our donors, at least 94 cents of that dollar went directly to the programs that benefit the kids. The remaining amount was used for the necessary operating expenses, so that the organization may continue to operate.

However, we have gone a major step further. For all those donors who wish to support a specific children's program, 100% of their donation goes to that program. We have ensured this accountability by establishing separate accounts for each of our programs. All specific program donations are directed to the chosen account. No general operating expenses are ever applied from these accounts.

No member of our Board of Directors has ever been paid a salary of any kind.

Without being conscious of it, I may have taken another page from my mentor Jesse White's standard operating procedure. For the first ten years, I simply operated the organization from my law office, and personally underwrote whatever expenses were required beyond that which was available. Over time, I too was persuaded the expansion of the organization would require broader support, and for the last ten years the organization has operated from an office that is separate from my law firm.

Dreams for Kids continues to operate in the spirit of our friend Jesse White and all those who support us—it's about the kids. Whatever is necessary, find a way to get it done to help the kids, and always respect the trust of those for whom we act.

Golfing for Dreams

Fundraising can be a difficult task. However, we have been fortunate to apply lessons learned from others relative to successful fundraising. If you want to raise funds and create awareness and have people show up at an event, you must have a good cause. If you want them to come back, you need to throw a good party.

The reality is most people want to be involved. The key is creating events to match their interests. One of our organizations historical trademarks has been the ability to attract those who wish to host events on our behalf. This gives people the opportunity to bring their friends together in a way that interests them and use that opportunity to raise funds for the kids. It also introduces an entirely new group of people to the Dreams for Kids' mission.

We have had individuals and groups of people who have hosted annual events for our kids for years. One such group is the Jeff Lawless Foundation, which was established in memory of a young man who died in an accident one week prior to his wedding. Jeff was an avid volleyball player, as were his friends. Their annual volleyball tournament became our volleyball tournament as well, and it gives those who love the beach and the sun an opportunity to be involved. It also gives us a day to remember Jeff Lawless.

Our plan is to bring a group of children with disabilities to the tournament and introduce them to volleyball. This will be the perfect marriage. A group of donors, having a great time, while raising funds and awareness for kids in need—and the kids themselves. The donors will see and feel the results of their generosity and, better yet, can work directly with the kids and receive all of the personal rewards such an experience always gives.

Early on we discovered the obvious: a lot of people like to golf. I may not be one of them, but I respect the huge following that the game has. So our very first year we hosted a golf outing. The Annual Dreams for Kids' Golf Outing, now in its 20th year, has been the place where golfers can also be introduced to Dreams.

The day itself has been everything a great golf outing can be and so much more. We make sure the day on the golf course is an absolute treat, but the real reward comes later, after dinner, when our program brings home our true spirit.

For the first few years, the dinner that followed golf was simply a time to meet with old friends and trade exaggerated scores and other fish tales. One year, we decided that we should introduce our golfers and dinner guests to a program, which gave them an opportunity to experience the results of their generosity. This decision connected our donors to the true intent of the day and elevated Dreams for Kids to a level of giving that expanded in ways we had never imagined.

A Whole New World

I took the road less traveled by, and that has made all the difference.

~ Robert Frost

Prior to our introduction to J.J. O'Connor, our organization hadn't truly been aware of the world of those with disabilities.

Our mission had been to serve kids who were disadvantaged, for which there was never a shortage of worthy recipients. However, we were missing a sadly hidden and isolated part of our society. Nearly invisible as they struggled to find access to everyday life, were thousands and thousands of children living with a disability.

Through J.J. and others, we learned of the deep isolation that children with disabilities feel. One day, by focusing our attention on these children, Dreams for Kids was elevated as an organization and elevated the lives of our volunteers who connected with those children through our programs.

However, in the summer of 1997, none of this was even a dream. Then, a few weeks prior to our golf outing, an article appeared in a small suburban newspaper.

The article was written about a young man, a letter, and a boy in Cambodia. There was something about this story that captivated the spirit. In reading the article, I had an unmistakable feeling of being introduced to something special. It was one of those moments where every instinct tells you that there is great change ahead. I had no way of knowing what was in store, but I do remember smiling.

As we prepared for our 8th Annual Dreams for Kids' Golf Outing, we felt the anticipation one feels before a great transition in life.

11

J.J. Ropes Us In

It's not the mountain we conquer, but ourselves.

~ Edmund Hillary

In the summer of 1997, during Dreams for Kids eighth year, one of our Board members brought an article to our Director's meeting. The article was written about a young man who, at seventeen years of age, had entered a writing contest. The contest was sponsored by the religious order of priests in his high school. The intent was to choose the best letter among all the students participating and to award that student $500. The purpose of the letter was to encourage a little boy in Cambodia who had lost his legs in a land mine accident.

Helping to Heal

November 7, 1996
Dear Sok Thea,
Life can change drastically. One second you're going about your business and the next you're in the hospital starting a new life. I

recently read about your tragic experience, and the way it has dramatically changed your life. I am happy that you have found new hope with the school you are now attending. I hope and pray for you and your family, as you continue your life's journey through these difficult times.

I know a young man who has had to overcome some very difficult situations. He was happy with his life until suddenly it changed beyond his comprehension. At sixteen-years-old, he went out one evening to play ice hockey, a sport he dearly loved. During the game, he was chasing the puck into a corner with a member of the opposing team, and they both fell and went crashing into the end boards. The opponent, who is a childhood friend, got up and skated away while he lay still on the ice. When he went into the boards, he broke his neck and became paralyzed from the neck down.

The night of his injury he was not expected to live. After the first night was over, he was not expected to make it through surgery. Following surgery, he was not expected to move from the neck down. Now one year later, he is finishing his senior year of high school and continuing daily therapy. He is able to stand and take a few steps with assistance. He has come so far, but still has a long journey ahead of him.

Throughout all of this, his family, like yours, has been with him every step of the way. A few of his friends have stayed by his side through his ordeal while many have faded away. He has also made a few new friends along the way. He has learned much from his experiences. He knows what it is like to face the odds head on and rely on inner strength, determination, and God to see him through this battle. I know so much about this young man because I am he. I have felt many emotions since the time of the injury and am sure you have as well. I have feelings of worthlessness, fear, and happiness, just to name a few. Some days are harder than others, but the key is to not let the down days override the positive ones. I am sure God is watching and is with me every step of the way, and I believe he is also watching over you. I am a firm believer that if you do your best, God will take care of the rest.

During the past summer, I had the opportunity to visit the highest mountain in North America, Pikes Peak. From the moment I stepped off the airplane, I was mesmerized by this immense wonder of nature. I was in Colorado for a week and it wasn't until the last day that I could visit the top of Pikes Peak. This left a lasting impression that I will carry with me the rest of my life. As I stood at the top of the Peak looking over the mountains, I could not help but wonder why fate had dealt me these cards. How could God who loves me so much let this happen? If God has so much power, why can't he reverse what happened? I was a good person before my mishap and did not feel I deserved this misfortune. I don't believe anyone deserves such a punishment. I asked myself these questions over and over and probably will ask them for the rest of my life.

The one truth I have learned is that we all have our own mountain to climb. Some may have smaller mountains while others have much larger ones, but each has their own to climb. These mountains represent your goals and the hardships you must conquer. The rope you will use to climb your mountain is your family and friends, through the love and understanding they provide. This rope will support and catch you if you fall, but can never do the climbing for you. To reach the top of your mountain requires strength, courage and determination, all attributes that come straight from the heart and soul. To stand at the top of your mountain, you will see what you have conquered and know that you have achieved your dream. Not only do you stand at the top of your mountain, but you stand closest to God.

I hope that the journey up your mountain is filled with love and compassion. I believe you have the will to reach the top and you must believe the same. God is looking over your shoulder and will never give up on you, as long as you never give up on Him. I will continue to pray for you and your family each day as we continue our journeys together.

Sincerely,

J.J. O'Connor

Would it be a surprise to find out that J.J. won the letter writing contest? As he was presented his check for $500, he gave it back.

J.J. told the priests to give the check to Sok Thea, "That boy needs it more than I do."

Do you ever reflect on the choices you have made and how your life may have been different if you had chosen differently? While it is best not to spend too much time in that place, it is fascinating to think of all that transpires for an individual or an organization, and in this case, for thousands of children and their families because of a single choice.

I remember sitting at my desk when I first read J.J.'s letter to Sok Thea. I am sure my reaction was much the same as yours. I was moved and I was also grateful to have been given the letter. Fortunately, it did not take any convincing for the Board to unanimously decide that we had to honor this young man, and that his presence would make for a special evening at our golf outing.

However, most people never knew how close we were to never having met J.J., who told me years later that he was not planning on accepting our invitation. He said he was unsure as to why we had invited him to our event, and because he did not know anyone associated with our organization, his initial reaction was to politely decline. J.J. also said he really did not know why he was being honored and what he had done to deserve it.

Once again it was a mother's advice that set the course and direction for the future of Dreams for Kids. J.J.'s mom, Blanche O'Connor, persuaded him that he should accept our invitation, and together they attended the Dreams for Kids 8th Annual Golf Outing.

A Generous Spirit

When the game is over, the king and pawn go back in the same box.

~ Irish saying

What compelled us to honor J.J. was not the disability he had suffered. Instead, our choice was made based on the spirit he so obviously possessed. Suffering as he was, at such a young age, he had chosen to encourage and to help someone else. For a young man to also decide to return a check was something that spoke volumes of his character. We discovered that this decision was even more remarkable since his family was one of modest means. J.J. has five sisters and his injury forced his mother and father to do all they could just to make ends meet.

The remarkable mentors of Dreams for Kids; Jesse, Father Wally, and Clara all shared one unbreakable rule: *Those who receive other's help must give back to the next person.* The circle of giving must forever remain unbroken. We were introduced to a young man who had suffered physical paralysis, yet had still maintained the ability and desire to help someone else who was in greater need. In turn, J.J. introduced us to the world of disability, and it was shocking to find out just how isolated that world could be.

When J.J. arrived the night of our golf outing dinner, most of those present, including myself, were not at all prepared. It is, unfortunately, very common for many people to have little exposure to someone with a disability. There is a distance that exists, and as we learned and grew as an organization it became our mission to lessen that distance.

There is a unique aspect to J.J.'s disability, as there is to most others who have suffered disability by injury. At one time, he was as able-bodied as those who golfed that afternoon were, and in most cases even more so. J.J. was an athlete. He was in the prime of his youth and was in peak physical condition. One second later, he was paralyzed from the neck down.

J.J. also was a good-looking eighteen-year-old kid, with an engaging smile and a personality to match. None of this was taken away when he was injured. For all outward appearances, here was the same eighteen-year-old athlete, sitting in a wheelchair, completely paralyzed. It was a sobering reminder of how all of our lives can change in an instant.

The greater lesson we learned over time is that, no matter what the outward appearances may be and no matter what the physical or developmental disability is, there is a person in that chair, just like you and me.

When the time came to introduce J.J. to the overflow dinner crowd, there wasn't a sound to be heard. The anticipation had been building since J.J. arrived with his mom. Everyone wondered how the presentation would go and what affect it would have. Had we actually known how the night would unfold, we all would have just started crying right then and there.

I was to introduce J.J. In preparing to tell his story, I had devised a plan to keep my emotions in check, thinking it best to keep it together out of respect to the young man who was to follow me, as well as for the rest of the crowd. Well, that plan was about as effective as our parasailing plan would prove to be in Mexico.

I usually spent the day carting around the course, rather than golfing, to spend time with our supporters. One guest I frequently encountered on the course was particularly cranky; a big bear of a guy, beard and all, who never once cracked a smile. Well, there he was right in front of the spot where I was to introduce J.J. He was the perfect prop. I would just look at him when I was speaking. If that did not hold my emotions in check, plan B was to turn and look toward a Board member at the next table, who could be best described as a classic Chicago guy: tough, non-emotional, about 6'4", and a biscuit shy of 300 pounds.

Well, with J.J. right next to me, three lines into my introduction, the big bear's beard started filling up with tears. So, in an attempt to hang on to any hope that I would maintain my composure, I turned to the next table. There was Plan B, his face covered by his napkin. So much for my perfect plan.

After managing to get through my part, J.J. followed with a moving tribute to us all and emotionally thanked us for now being part of his *rope*. At that point, all tears broke loose, and everyone allowed the moment to be what it was.

Dreams for Kids had taken a monumental step toward our future, and what a future it would prove to be.

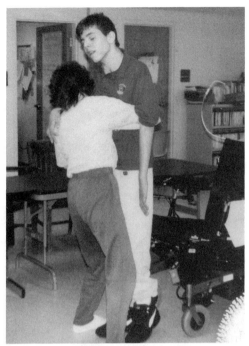

J.J. O'Connor 1995.
After nearly seven months of hospitalization,
J.J. is assisted to feet by his therapist Vicky to
attempt his first step towards his new life.

J.J. O'Connor 2004.
Moving with his special grace across the stage, J.J.
speaks professionally to 1,500 people at the annual
Allegra Print and Imaging Convention.

Jesse White Tumblers soar to their dreams.

Jesse White, Jim Smith, Tom Tuohy, J.J., journalist and long time friend Bill Kurtis celebrating the 45th Anniversary of the Jesse White Tumblers.

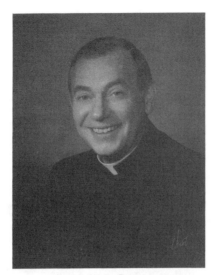

Father Wally Brennan.

"Pup" walks the streets of the Westside and meets
a friend, in a neighborhood full of Brennans.

The first Christmas, December 24, 1989, Clara's House.
Clara Kirk, with Bill Nolan, Jim "Plan B" Davern and Tom Tuohy.

Dreams for Kids Christmas, 1993,
Patricia Tuohy, Tom Tuohy, Kathleen Tuohy, and Heather Mix.

The Dream Team – Volunteers Christmas 2004.

"I'm 3 years old Santa"

Santa's seven ton Sleigh and 3,000 gifts, compliments of the United States Marines.

Holiday for Hope Chicago.

Holiday for Hope Cameroon.

Holiday for Hope Nigeria.

Holiday for Hope India.

Holiday for Hope Uganda.

Sgt. Richard Marak, remembering the kids of Iraq.

New Orleans Saints Pierre Thomas, making a difference.

On October 4, 1979, as his dolphin friend, Chicago Police
Officer Jim Zwit, looks on, eight year old Bobby Lujano is blessed
by Pope John Paul II in Holy Name Cathedral, Chicago Illinois.

2004 Summer Paralympic Games. Bob Lujano, competes for Team USA.

"I'll always be your Valentine." Carmen with her friend Michael.

23, Michael Jordan, takes a rare break from a Chicago Bulls game as his friend, Carmen Villafane, keeps an eye on the court.

Matthew on Bangs Lake, Illinois, "I'm a Water Skier Mom!"

Brendan on outrigger skis on Twin Lakes, Wisconsin.

Alexis on the golf range.

Courtney on the slopes.

Jonathan on the course.

Learning to fly with Diveheart.

"The Kiss."

Harlan and ICRE, making history.

Dream Leaders, Pavle of Serbia and Cortez of Chicago.

Tyler, helping us see the best in ourselves.

J.J. and his best friend, Dick Marak;
Spring Break, Puerto Vallarta
Mexico, the morning after
the kiss of a dolphin.

J.J.'s 'guardian angel,' the
uncommon man, Jim Smith, keeps
his constant watch over J.J.'s shoulder.

12

Jim Smith—
An Uncommon Man

*Everyone should carefully observe which way his heart
draws him, and then choose that way with all his
strength.*

~ Hasidic Proverb

I t has been said that once a person commits to following their
heart, the people who are required for the journey show up
on their path. The same can be said for Dreams for Kids. As
we now moved into uncharted waters and into the world of disabilities, we did not have to look far for our next magnificent role
model.

After meeting J.J., we learned of someone whose dedication and determination to assist J.J. was the stuff of legends. He
truly is an uncommon man. Ironically, he has the most common
of names, Jim Smith.

In October of 1995, on a cold and wintry day, Jim Smith
awoke early, not knowing his life would never be the same. He
had heard of a player who had been injured playing hockey.

Jim felt he had to visit this young man in an official capacity as Secretary of USA Hockey. As a newspaper reporter observed at the time, there was no indication in that first hospital room visit between Jim Smith and J.J. O'Connor that this meeting would forever change both of their lives.

As J.J. lay paralyzed in the hospital bed those first few days, his neck broken and barely coherent, he was surrounded by a complex mass of tubes keeping him alive. His family was ever present. A week after J.J. was injured Jim Smith arrived. This was an official visit for Jim and the most difficult of tasks. Jim was an elected representative of the Board of USA Hockey and he had a lifelong love for the game. To visit a young man whose life had been forever changed playing the game Jim so revered was heartbreaking.

All amateur hockey, including the Olympics, is governed by USA Hockey. This means the equipment, the players and referees, the regulations, are all managed by this single organization. Consequently, Jim is immediately made aware when an area high school athlete has suffered a serious hockey injury. As it turned out, when Jim was notified of J.J.'s injury, he lived only one town away from him.

On that first visit, Jim simply left his business card on a table in J.J.'s hospital room. Jim had spoken briefly to him and told J.J. to call him at anytime and that he would be there for him. There was no recognition, in that brief moment in time, of what the future would hold.

The following day, Jim returned to J.J.'s hospital room. Jim visited the day after that as well, and the next and the next. As J.J. recalls, sometimes Jim would whistle so loudly that he could hear him approaching from way down the hallway.

Jim Smith told J.J., who was lying in the most vulnerable state that can be imagined, with his devastated family as witnesses, that he would always be there for him and that he would see him every day. In a story that would be hard to believe had I not witnessed it, twenty years later, Jim Smith has kept his word.

He has not missed a single day. Jim Smith and J.J. O'Connor's lives are intertwined in wondrous ways.

"He's like another brother," Jim said. "You just looked at those eyes and you could tell the strength and courage he has." He recalled, "I just knew I was going to help him. He's pretty remarkable. He has never once said, 'Why me?'"

As days turned into weeks, and weeks turned into months, Jim served in the capacity of brother, physical aide, and best friend. He began helping J.J. with day-to-day tasks. He became such a central figure in J.J.'s life that their story almost seems beyond belief. Jim would take J.J. and his girlfriend to the movies. He would take him shopping or swimming, or any other place a young man might have wanted to go.

Soon enough, Jim filled in where J.J.'s parents could not, and quickly became a welcome member of the family.

Beyond Official Capacity

There is no traffic jam along the extra mile.
~ Roger Staubach

Jim had previously visited injured players before as part of his official responsibilities. He had devoted all of his spare time to Illinois youth hockey and also to his national and international responsibilities with USA Hockey and the Olympics. Jim was the successful owner and operator of two businesses and was a self-confessed workaholic. Still, he showed up at J.J.'s bedside every single day.

All the while, J.J. was observing a guy who was an undeniable creature of habit. He recalled that Jim would walk into his room every single day and always attempt to hang his coat on an invisible hook. As the coat would fall to the floor, Jim would do a double take, as if it had never happened before, and look around to see where he could hang his coat. Then Jim would proceed to tell some corny joke that made J.J. and any family members laugh and not necessarily because it was funny. Jim's routine became a welcome relief from the sorrow and the pain, and was an opportunity to smile through the tears.

Days were now rolling by, and Jim continued to show up. J.J. recalls, "I was sixteen-years-old and thrown into a situation that was just unbearable and devastating. I was not ready for this. My family was not ready. Jim walked in, told corny jokes and made us smile. For a family that was down and out, Jim was what we needed. He took me and showed me the way."

Hockey can have a reputation of being a dangerous, sometimes violent sport. The injuries range from cuts and bruises, to paralysis, and even death. Were Jim's official visits an effort to make amends for the consequences of playing the game? Were they an effort to control the media's portrayal of the sport? Did Jim take his role seriously in his stated belief that the hockey community is a family? Or, did he simply have nothing better to do?

For a while J.J. wondered, "What's his motivation? Anybody would. After you got to know him you realized Jim was just a guy who wanted to help." From that point on, Jim and J.J. became friends.

Jim said he knew that J.J. and his family were in no condition psychologically or financially to tackle what lay ahead. He had a distinct feeling that he needed to be there for them. It was as if Jim Smith had found his calling. To this day, he cannot explain why he felt so compelled to help J.J.

J.J. once remarked that he felt guilty about benefiting from Jim's continued assistance. However, he felt better about the situation after he came to realize that he was helping Jim to have a more meaningful life. J.J. was made aware of this when Jim's long time friend Norm Spiegel, and fellow USA Hockey official, told him that before Jim had met J.J., he only did one thing in life aside from hockey—he worked. J.J. realized that he had given him the opportunity to have a life after work and hockey, and he had given him someone to love.

Jim never had a son of his own. As he has helped J.J. continue on in life, J.J. has helped Jim find deeper meaning in his own life. In ways that are hard to explain unless you have met him, J.J. motivates and inspires people who encounter him. As for Jim Smith, the world is a far better place with a man of his character living in it.

Steve Smith, Jim's younger brother, observes, "Hockey has been Jim's family for the last twenty-five or more years." Steve and Jim are two of twelve siblings who grew up in a tight-knit family from Park Ridge, a suburb northwest of Chicago. "My brother Jim had no time for anything else. Now Jim's got a family. I think he's got that emotional happiness that he never really had before."

In those critical early days, as J.J. lay in his hospital bed, Jim rallied behind the scenes to encourage the hockey community to support him. Chicago Blackhawk players showed up at his bedside. If he said he was thirsty, a case of Gatorade suddenly arrived. Later, Jim showed up with a case of pickles, one of J.J.'s favorite foods.

You might think that such a meddler would eventually have a strained relationship with J.J.'s parents. This however did not happen. His parents soon realized that Jim's participation in their son's life was a blessing. In short order, they recognized that Jim was able to expand J.J.'s possibilities in ways that did not seem feasible for someone with his severe injuries.

J.J.'s father, Terry O'Connor, admits to having had mixed feelings as Jim became a fixture in his son's life. However, Terry now marvels, "Jim would come in to the hospital room and while J.J. was still on a respirator, Jim would have all of us laughing." J.J.'s mother, Blanche, recalls, "We were thinking, who is this guy? He was there to help. He was there, and he was there, and he was there. I asked him once, 'Don't you have a home?' I think he simply took J.J. under his wing, and we thank God for that."

One night, after he had been transferred from Evanston

Hospital to the Rehabilitation Institute of Chicago, J.J. mentioned a craving for a hot, juicy steak. The very next day, Jim and his brother Steve showed up with a grill and cooked for the Rehabilitation Institute of Chicago's entire fifth floor. The wind chill factor that evening was 30 degrees below zero. J.J. laughs as he remembers watching from the hospital room window as the two men huddled under a lamppost with smoke pouring out of the grill. Later that day, Jim and Steve smuggled in steaks to feed all the patients on the floor.

"It was the best steak I have ever had," J.J. said.

When J.J. got out of the hospital, Jim brought him to a Blackhawk's hockey game and introduced him to Bill Wirtz, the legendary owner of the Blackhawk's team and United Center. Jim also brought J.J. to the USA Hockey meetings, which led to J.J. being elected as a director for the organization. J.J. is now in charge of disabled hockey for the country, is general manager of the gold-medal USA 2010 Paralympic Sled Hockey Team, and founder of the Chicago Hornets Sled Hockey Team.

Now the Real Work Begins

To the world you may be one person, but to one person you may be the world.

~ Anonymous

As mentioned, after his hospitalization J.J. continued therapy at Marianjoy Rehabilitation Hospital in Wheaton, Illinois. The drive took ninety minutes each way.

Early on, Jim recognized that because of their work schedule, it would be difficult for J.J.'s parents to transport him to therapy. J.J.'s parents worked different shifts and were relieved when Jim offered to drive their son. It was during those long treks that Jim and J.J.'s friendship deepened.

As time passed, Jim began to stay later into the evenings

at the O'Connor house. Jim would help lift and bathe J.J. and exercise his limbs. With J.J.'s father working most evenings and his mother having all she could handle with her five daughters, Jim knew he could be of help.

After returning to high school and graduating from Loyola Academy, J.J. was accepted at Lake Forest College. He received scholarships from both Lake Forest College and from the Chicago Blackhawk Alumni. With the beginning of college and the many challenges J.J. would face, Jim arranged to hire a childhood pal of J.J.'s, a young man by the name of Jamil Herezi, to help J.J. during the day. For the first two years, J.J. commuted to school in a special vehicle. Jamil would drive him to college, take notes for him during his classes, and then drive him to RIC for therapy before returning home.

One day Jim asked J.J. how he was doing. J.J. confessed that he felt he was missing out on the full college experience. He said that being pushed into class and back to the van wasn't allowing him to have the type of fun experiences and relationships that most college kids had. It was at that moment that Jim's spirit and boundless commitment rose to an occasion few could imagine. Jim said, "Why not move into the dorms?" When J.J. replied with a puzzled look, "How in the heck would I manage that?" Jim simply replied, "We'll figure out a way." Jim Smith repeated the words he had spoken to J.J. before, words he would say time and time again, "We'll make it work."

Knowing that there would be no one to take care of J.J. during what the family refers to as "the night shift," Jim shrugged his shoulders and said, "I'll just move into the dorms with you." On seeing the look of complete disbelief on J.J.'s face, Jim quickly stated, "I always wanted to go back to school again anyway." Yes, Jim Smith moved into the dorms. Keep in mind, not only was it a college dorm, but the "night shift" involved getting up several times a night to assist J.J.

When someone is paralyzed, they do not lose the urge to toss and turn in the night just like able-bodied people do every night in their sleep. Repositioning during sleep rarely awakens someone who is able to move. The problem for a paralyzed person is that they have lost the unconscious ability to reposition themselves, and as they lie motionless, the urge and inability to move awakens them and they may become claustrophobic. Whoever is available within earshot has to wake up and move the paralyzed person's arm or leg or reposition the person's body in bed. This may happen three to five times a night or more. Add the person's other basic needs to this, and the "night shift" often includes everything but a good night's sleep.

Now half way through J.J.'s junior year, Jim's amazing dedication to him gave J.J. a new lease on the entire college experience. As J.J. describes, "Jim gave me a chance to be a college kid, and not just someone taking classes."

Many of Jim's friends wondered how this arrangement would work out. Jim's friend Norm said, "We were concerned in the beginning, because of the time he was devoting to J.J. On the other hand, there is nobody else like Jim." As Jim noted, "Being single and owning my own business, I'm pretty much free to do what I want." What Jim Smith wanted to do is what separates him from the ordinary person. He saw a life that could be lived, and lived well, if only doors could be opened and limitations taken away. He captured that vision and made it reality. Jim Smith was the very essence of a dolphin.

Fortunately, Lake Forest College had just finished building a wheelchair-accessible residence hall, which contained larger, apartment-like suites. Half-jokingly, Jim said that the only way he'd move in was if he could bring in a television and was allowed cable access. Of course the large screen television ended up in the living room and became the place to hang out for the kids on campus. No place for the medical and rehabilitation workout equipment and treadmill? Jim's bedroom would be fine. Jim shrugged and said, "All I need is room for my bed." Eventually, J.J. and Jim shared their apartment-like suite with another college student. They equipped their "crib" with the 60-inch satellite television, a stereo system, two refrigerators, sofa, two Lazy Boys, convection oven, and even carpeting.

Home away from Home

During the day, while Jim was at work, Jamil assisted J.J. Members of the college hockey team also helped him work out every day after class on equipment that helped increase blood flow to his legs. Later, Jim read to J.J. each night from class textbooks, wrote the words J.J. chose for school papers, studied along with him for every single test, and literally "went to college himself for a second time" to ensure fulfillment of J.J.'s outstanding scholarship.

Setting aside all thought of himself, Jim dedicated almost every minute of his time to ensuring that J.J. enjoyed the full college experience and had an active social life. When there was a function on campus that J.J. wanted to attend Jim "made it work." If J.J. wanted to go out for the evening, Jim would take him to the event and ask him when he wanted to be picked up. Then, even if it was 1:00 a.m. or much later, Jim would swing by, get him and bring him back to the dorm room. When J.J. met and dated women during college, and indeed he was not deprived of admiring females, once again, Jim made it possible for J.J. to live life, just like all of the other kids.

Jim became something of a legend on campus. He seemed to be everywhere and yet he was invisible at the same time. Whenever needed, for whatever reason, at whatever time, Jim would suddenly appear, and then fade into the background, making sure that it was J.J.'s scene. Driving the van, picking up the pizzas, waiting in the parking lot, folding clothes in the laundry room; whatever it took, Jim would fill the role. The students on campus even affectionately referred to him as "The Butler." As if he had not already done so, Jim Smith cemented his reputation as one extraordinary guy.

Uncommonly Connected

There are two types of people—those who come into a room and say, "Well, here I am!" and those who come in and say, "Ah, there you are."

~ Frederick L. Collins

Over time, this extremely uncommon man with the most common of names, Jim Smith has proven to be one of the most committed, energetic, and passionate people you could ever hope to meet. Yet none of this comes across. Jim certainly would not tell you and you would have an impossible time prying any self-recognition out of him. Jim simply recognizes the tremendous value of human connection and service to others and making good things happen. Jim seeks no reward, yet has acknowledged he has received more than he has given. Jim Smith regards his association with J.J. O'Connor as the gift of a lifetime.

At one of Dreams for Kids' annual golf outing dinners, a few years after we met this extraordinary man, we chose to directly honor Jim Smith as our first "Unsung Hero." That night, I introduced Jim and said, in part:

...Jim Smith has studied for every single test, term paper, and school project that J.J. was required to complete since he was a senior student at Loyola Academy through his current studies at Lake Forest College, where, incidentally J.J. is an A student, majoring in business administration.

Every night, Jim holds the book J.J. needs to read. Jim writes the words that J.J. wishes to be written. Jim performs every task for him that many of us take for granted in our everyday lives, such as combing J.J.'s hair and brushing his teeth, giving him his bath, dressing him and tying his shoes. All this and more, Jim does for J.J.

A couple of days ago, I spoke to J.J. about this award for Jim. The honor he is about to receive is a surprise to Jim Smith. Jim had absolutely no idea he was to be honored. I asked J.J. for an example of what Jim Smith does for him.

J.J. told of an example of what Jim does every single day. He said he was attending a Sunday night concert with friends and got back to his house very late. As J.J. tells it, "I woke up the next morning and my clothes were laid out and my medicine was next to my bed and my backpack was filled for school. Jim Smith had been there while I was asleep."

J.J. has said of Jim Smith, "He is my Guardian Angel."

As J.J. says, "It's amazing how this guy could get in his car four years ago and upon seeing this kid he had never laid eyes on before, tell him, 'I'll stick with you and you're gonna make it.' Four years later, he sees to this promise every single day...."

Ladies and gentlemen, please help us honor Jim Smith....

As Jim rose to face a standing ovation that no man has earned more, J.J. had a chance to pay tribute to his friend:

I thought long and hard about what I need to say to thank this man. There is not one word I can say to all of you today that would help you understand how important Jim Smith is to me and what a wonderful person he is. I cannot do it.

I could probably thank everybody in this room for one thing or another. I can thank you for listening to me tonight. I don't know how to thank Jim. It's impossible. How could somebody just walk into my room and dedicate his entire life to me? Why am I so lucky? What did I do to deserve Jim Smith in my life? I still can't figure it out. I wish I could help everyone understand. I wish I understood.

It's not only that Jim is there every single night to help me with my homework. It's that I know, no matter what day of the week it is, if I'm not having a good day, and I have a tear rolling down my cheek, Jim is always going be the one with the tissue to wipe my face. Jim Smith is going to make sure that before I go to bed that night, I am going to be smiling.

Jim Smith is the reason I can sit here in front of you tonight and smile. He is the reason that Tom and others can have good things to say about me. Jim is the one that taught me that anything anyone can do, I can do too. I am so thankful for what this man does for me.

I know it doesn't matter what anybody else thinks of you. It's what you feel inside that really counts. People have said that I'm very inspirational. People have come up to me and said, "Wow, how do you do what you do?" I say this: I wouldn't be able to do anything if not for Jim. The only thing I know for certain is that someday when I grow up, I hope to be just like Jim Smith.

Is it any surprise that Jim Smith now organizes our entire Christmas Party? As is his incomparable nature, one year he just took charge; volunteer lists, nametags, job responsibilities, wrap party, printing, bags, walkie-talkies; he does it all. We call him the "General" and believe me, he has earned that rank.

As the years have gone by, now nearly thirteen years in all, I marvel at the consistency and unwavering dedication of Jim Smith. I look at his life and his relationship with J.J. as an astounding story. I look at him and what I see is a modern day hero. Jim Smith is truly a remarkably uncommon man for the ages.

It's a comfort to know there are heroes among us— regular people, just like you—willing to do what they can to make the world a better place. Heroes give instead of take. They act instead of talk. They step forward and do the hard and unseen jobs. To give the best of themselves, measuring their own success not by wealth or comfort, but by the lives they touch along the way. That's what heroes do and you are one of those people. Maybe you don't think of yourself that way but that's what you are. And I just want to tell you how grateful I am to know you and to know that there are heroes like you in the world.

~ J.F. Peterson

When it comes to family, it is said "apples don't fall far from the tree." Nothing could be truer when it comes to the Smith family. When we met the hero that is Jim Smith, we wondered if there could be another person like him. We did not have to look far for the answer.

13

Dick Marak—
A Marine Who
Leads with His Heart

If you want happiness for an hour, take a nap. If you want happiness for a day, go fishing. If you want happiness for a year, inherit a fortune. If you want happiness for a lifetime, help somebody.

~ Chinese Proverb

When Dreams for Kids met J.J. O'Connor, his unique presence would shine light on a new direction for our organization. However, Jim Smith is the shining example of how one person can make a difference in another's life. We soon realized that there was a younger version of Jim Smith, and his name is Dick Marak. This young man blessed us with a living example that helped shape the future mission of our organization.

You may remember that Dick is the friend of J.J. who was a part of the Puerto Vallarta experience. Dick was also the person holding J.J. for the extraordinary kiss of a dolphin. I learned that there were more than two dolphins in the pool that day in Mexico. My life and the lives of thousands of kids have been made so much richer, by being graced by this dolphin's life.

If there ever was an example of what an adult could accomplish in the life of someone in need, it is the ultimate role model, Jim Smith. To understand how much a young person can also profoundly affect the lives of others, one needs to look no further than Dick Marak.

Dick Marak is Jim Smith's nephew. As with great athletes, it can be all too easy to assume that the greatness in them is a gift primarily born of great genes. However, Dick's stepfather is Jim's brother. There is no blood relation. I cannot help but think that Dick was raised around the same guiding principles with which Jim was raised. That type of influence and upbringing gives us all hope. If they were just born this way, the rest of us would have a heck of a time catching up.

Dick learned about J.J from his Uncle Jim. Dick was only sixteen when Jim told him about the hockey player that he had visited in the hospital. Dick remembers Jim telling him that he and J.J. were the same age, and he was aware that his uncle had returned to visit J.J. daily.

One day Dick told his uncle that he would like to meet J.J. Dick and J.J. were both seniors in high school and Dick simply said, "Ask the kid if he would like to hang out sometime."

From the time of that very first request to the present day, there has never been a time when Dick has considered what he has done to be an obligation or anything special or out of the ordinary. For many it might have been, especially at that age, but Dick is a young man who simply acts out of instinct and in the most natural way. J.J. was his age, and maybe they would have something in common. "I thought that since J.J. was my age, maybe we would like some of the same things and might become friends. I have never looked at him as being any different from me and I still do not," he says today.

If we consider the tragic possibility that one of our lifelong friends is injured in an accident and is now paralyzed, ideally the friendship remains intact and it may even be strengthened. As J.J. has painfully and sadly related to me, the reality has proven to be quite different. He says that nearly all of the friends he had when he was able-bodied were less inclined to remain friends with him once he suffered his injury. Most disappeared completely. He says this can be quite common among others who suffer life-changing disabilities.

J.J.'s best friend, his constant buddy, never came to see him in the hospital after his injury. He has not called or seen J.J. since that day. I asked J.J. if this hurt him and he said yes, because they had talked about so many things that they were going to do together in the future. They seemed to have so much in common and had so much fun together. There never was much doubt in his mind that they would remain life-long friends.

I asked him what he would do if he saw that friend today. Using the limited ability he has to raise his right arm, he raised it slightly and said, "I'd give him a hug and tell him that I love him."

As we talked about this and other disappointments and the major adjustments in his life since his injury, J.J. said, "There is too much hurt in the world today. There is no point in letting what happened yesterday affect how you feel toward a person today if they want to be a part of your life again." When J.J. said this, there were tears in his eyes and I could feel the hurt.

Dick Marak was not a part of J.J.'s life before the accident. Dick became part of a new network of friends that he developed post injury. That network was built slowly and much differently than before. It is the reality that comes with people treating you differently even though you are really the same person, just physically different. Dick Marak was the exception to the rule. This new friendship endured for the most basic of reasons: He never treated J.J. any differently than any of his other friends.

What I have always found to be remarkable is that, prior to meeting J.J., Dick never really had known anyone who used a wheelchair or had a significant disability. None of this mattered, because he only thought of this kid he never met as being his age and not as being a quadriplegic. From the moment they met, Dick only saw the kid in the chair and not the chair.

"Do You Want To Go To A Party?"

We cannot hold a torch to light another's path without brightening our own.

~ Ben Sweetland

After meeting with J.J. and talking briefly, some time passed and Dick called J.J. on the phone and asked that question which never fails to get a positive response from a sixteen-year-old: "Do you want to go to a party?" We have a winner. I wonder if that request has ever been turned down by anyone that age. Consider a kid who has lost most of his world and all the people his own age. Imagine his feelings when given a chance to find it again.

Taking someone in a wheelchair to a party for the first time is a challenging experience. The logistics of transferring someone from their home, out the door, out of their chair and into a vehicle, out of the vehicle and into their chair, and into a house without accessibility modifications, requires being prepared for a little bit of work and a lot of adjustments. I did not know Dick at that time, but would have a hard time believing that he was any different than he is now. He just looks at any situation and finds a way to get it taken care of. However, even as Dick would have found a little work to be no problem at all, there is the reality of attending a party with someone who is different from all the rest of your teenage friends. It puts an entirely different spin on, "Who's the new guy?"

When J.J. recalls that day, he remembers it as a day that he was afraid would never return to his life, "I was really struggling at that time. Overnight, everyone in my life was an adult. I was surrounded by doctors and therapists, my parents and Jim. They saved my life, but I had lost all my friends and, literally, everyone my own age. I was not sure I would ever get that back again."

"It is difficult enough for anyone being sixteen-years-old. It is difficult to feel comfortable with yourself, which usually leads to uncomfortable situations around anyone your own age who you do not know. I was so nervous when Dick asked me to go to that party. I did not know whether the kids at the party would make fun of me, and I was afraid that they would take it out on Dick. I still had no idea if girls would ever like me again. On top of all that, I did not know Dick Marak. I did not know if his uncle had asked him to take this kid out to a party, or if he was just doing it as a one-time thing. A lot of people talked about doing things with me after I got hurt, but it did not happen. Dick actually did it. I was so nervous that night because so much had to work out for Dick to ever call me again, and the chances of that happening seemed pretty remote."

J.J. reflected with a sense of reverence, "Here is a kid my own age, who I did not know, who had to take on a situation that he was not at all familiar with, and risk being ridiculed by his friends for doing so. Dick had to drive one hour into the city just to pick me up. That meant he would drive at least four hours that night, just to bring me to a party."

"That night became the beginning of me being a kid again. Because of Dick, between the ages of eighteen and twenty-two, I would really end up doing whatever any other kid my age did. Dick Marak really changed my whole life."

The reception at the party was not as bad as J.J. feared, but it took some intervention to make it work. However, this was the first of countless times that Dick Marak rose to the dolphin occasion. He helped others accept J.J. for who he is. Whether they liked or related to him was all up to them, as long as the chair didn't get in the way. Dick jumped right into the deep end of the pool. With an uncommon, selfless attitude, he brought J.J. into his world.

Dancing Down Walls

Dick Marak has never lacked friends. In fact, he was one of the most popular kids in his high school and for all of the right reasons. Not surprisingly, meeting Dick's friends meant meeting a cross section of every group in high school. Bringing J.J. in was just a natural extension of who Dick already was. He certainly didn't feel sorry for J.J., nor did he feel he was doing anything special, which is what made it work. He was just an ordinary kid, doing the extraordinary, in a way that set an enduring example of how it is done.

I met Dick at a Dreams for Kids' fundraiser, not long after he had befriended J.J. This particular event had a dance floor and I remember standing next to Dick and J.J. when Dick, who does not spend much time standing still, suddenly said, "We've got to get this party started." With that, he just grabbed J.J. by his wheelchair and off they went to the dance floor. It was his custom to wheel J.J. out to the center of the floor so J.J. could meet people. Initially, no one would talk to J.J. If girls would ask him to dance, he would be ready to surprise them. Yes, the kid in the wheelchair could dance. It rarely happened. To this, Dick found a simple solution. He and J.J. would simply move to the center of the room and dance. If the party would not come to them, they would bring the dance to the party.

Dick is so secure in who he is, and has his act together so well, that stepping out onto an empty dance floor with another guy, a guy in a wheelchair, no less, was no problem for him. This is Dick's invitation for everyone else in the room to loosen up and have some fun. That night a funny thing happened on the way to an awkward moment. A party broke out. One by one, and with no hesitation, people filled the dance floor. People who were just waiting for someone to break the ice jumped in, but the floor also filled with characters I had never seen, or would I ever think of seeing on a dance floor. Remember that big tough Chicago guy that ended up with his face covered in a napkin during J.J.'s introduction? There he was, on the dance floor, doing the…I'm not sure what he was doing, but he was having a great time.

The phenomenal part of this scene is that everyone was surrounding J.J. and the chair became an invisible girl magnet. J.J. was not just sitting there either. He was busting out his patented moves, which he calls "the quad dance." This is basically J.J. moving his right arm up and forward, in a limited way, causing his shoulder to move forward and leaning into the music and back, and, it would be hard not to say, with some rhythm. What happened that night, I witnessed time and time again, and I witnessed it in three different countries around the world.

It was remarkable to see it for the first time and it has been remarkable to participate in every time. J.J. is just having fun, and maybe even forgetting about his own chair. Dick is representing the very best in all of us, by allowing someone who would otherwise be isolated from the rest of the crowd, and probably not even be in the crowd, to now become the most popular person in the room. Dick Marak is a dolphin of the highest order.

Leading from the Heart

Great hearts steadily send forth the secret forces that incessantly draw great events.
~ Ralph Waldo Emerson

More than anyone I know, Dick Marak leads with his heart. He would wave that one off if you brought it up because he would be embarrassed to hear it and also because this is the only way that he knows how to live. It is nevertheless true, and especially for someone of his age, rather remarkable. With the ever present prospect of peer pressure and the desire to be an accepted part of a group, he has consistently shown the character and maturity to follow the beat of his own drum and has always timed it to the beat of his heart.

The very first time I met Dick, he enthusiastically asked what he could do to be involved in Dreams for Kids. Not surprisingly, he loved the idea of the organization and really wanted to be part of it. Since that day, Dick Marak has proven to be one of the most effective and committed volunteers in our twenty-year history. Today, he continues to serve Dreams for Kids in extraordinary ways.

If it was two o'clock in the morning, and I was in a jam and needed somebody to call, Dick is the first person to whom I would reach out. He is the only person I would need to call because he would respond immediately, without even asking questions, until he was there. If I have called him at two in the morning, I deny it ever happening, but will certainly admit to calling him more than a few times at 6:00 a.m. or at midnight. He was there in a heartbeat.

Whenever I discuss Dreams for Kids' business with Dick, even in passing, he wants to know how he fits in and when he will be needed.

On one occasion, I mentioned to Dick that we needed to raise funds quickly for a young man who was injured. His response was to mobilize his friends immediately. Within forty-eight hours, he and his friends raised the money required. In pouring rain, they took to the streets for a vehicle to vehicle fundraiser. He had turned the weather into a positive. Soaked to the skin, he called to say, "We are having a blast, and everyone feels so bad for us, they're lining up to donate!"

That is just one of the many memories I have of Dick that makes me smile. He never considers the conditions, only the objective and pursues the goal with an enthusiasm and work ethic, which are contagious. He opens doors, knocks down walls and leads others to a better place.

Just like the rest of us, Dick Marak is not a perfect person. He has his faults, which he would readily admit to, but he does the right thing so often, regardless of the conditions, that you have to stand back and marvel. His efforts in support of J.J. have had a tremendous impact on J.J.'s life. The greatest impact of all has been his friendship. Dick sees it quite simply: "I don't look at 'J' as being different. We have our differences, but we get past them. 'J' is my friend and I am his friend."

As good a friend as he was to J.J. and to so many others, Dick was in one of life's transitions and searching for some direction for his future. He was looking for something to do that gave him an opportunity to be challenged and to serve a purpose that could make a difference. He joined the United States Marine Corps. When he joined the Marines, he was as ready as one can be for what was to follow. In characteristic style, he actually appreciated boot camp. He is proud of doing what was necessary to have been trained to be a Marine, and being a Marine has impacted Dick in the best of ways.

Semper Fidelis

Wheresoever you go, go with all your heart.

~ Confucius

He is now Sgt. Marak of the United States Marines. The Marine Corps Values of Honor, Courage, and Commitment are in his blood. However, it can never be said that Dick had to adopt those values for they were already flowing through his veins. At boot camp, the Marines teach you to unpack the words *me, my, mine,* and prepare yourself to leave them behind, for you are now part of a team. Those words were never in Dick Marak's vocabulary. Semper Fidelis, the Marine Corps motto, translated from Latin, means *Always Faithful.* Dick Marak has lived his young life always faithful to the values that make a difference in the lives of others.

As he worked hard to earn his stripes, he also earned a position in the Corps which was a natural for him, namely, Field Coordinator of the Toys for Tots program in the Chicago area.

Since its inception in 1947, The Marine Corps Reserve

Toys for Tots Program has distributed over 320 million toys to needy children in every state in the Union. This program is one of the most outstanding traditions in the country, and it is an honor to be assigned to help coordinate the local efforts. Each year the Marines mobilize the community between October and Christmas, and deliver the distinctive Toys for Tots boxes to police stations, community centers, churches, local businesses and other organizations, for the toy collection to be given to the neediest of kids at Christmas.

When it comes to actually collecting toys, as you might guess, Dick is without peer. Whether at parties, other events or during the regular toy collection pick-up, he has consistently collected the most toys for our annual Christmas Party.

In 2005, Dick was personally responsible for the collection of over 3,000 toys just for the children of Dreams for Kids. This is in addition to the countless other tens of thousands he collected in his capacity with Toys for Tots. To just collect the toys would hardly be enough for a guy like Dick. He personally delivered all 3,000 gifts to our "wrap party," delivered 600 more toys for us to an area children's shelter, and returned to load 1,200 shopping bags full of gifts and candy in a truck and deliver them to the Dreams for Kids' Christmas Party location. When he arrived at our party site, he realized that we were short on trees. He immediately jumped back into his vehicle and found a dozen Christmas trees.

Based on what Dick Marak had done in the last ten years for Dreams for Kids, I wrote a letter of commendation to his U.S. Marine Corps Commanding Officer, which follows:

Dear Sir,

I am writing this letter as commendation for Lance Corporal Richard Marak and in appreciation for all he has done for our organization to assist children for the past ten years.

Lance Corporal Marak has dedicated himself tirelessly and unconditionally to our cause for more than a decade. Since he was a very young man he has looked out for others and has unconditionally given service to those less fortunate. He is one of the finest young men that I know and I am deeply grateful for all that he has done and for how he has conducted himself as a role model.

Lance Corporal Marak has recently assisted our efforts through his Marine Corps Reserve work with Toys for Tots, and thanks to his daily assistance, we have been able to reach out to more children this holiday season than ever before in our sixteen-year history. Lance Corporal Marak has given our effort a sense of discipline, honor and integrity that speaks volumes of the Marines and he is a credit to his uniform, and to the principles that his training and service have instilled in him.

I have seen him grow as a man in the Corps and I commend you and all of your fellow officers and superiors for the influence that you have had in his development.

Thank you for allowing Lance Corporal Marak to lend his time to our effort, and thank you for all the work the United States Marines do to make every Holiday Season brighter for those children in need of hope.

Gratefully,
Tom Tuohy
President, Dreams for Kids

In response to this letter and in recognition of his many other contributions to the community, and in acknowledgment of his outstanding character, Lance Corporal Marak was awarded the Marine Corps highest honor for community service. It was a very proud moment for me to be asked to take part in the official ceremony on the Marine Base, and to be given the honor of addressing his Marine Unit and officially "pinning" then Lance Corporal Richard Marak.

Dick continues to be involved in the community and with Dreams for Kids in the most remarkable and valuable of ways. He has also maintained his close friendship with J.J. and the two recently opened several Sport Clips franchises. Wherever he is and whatever he is doing, it can be certain that Dick Marak is leading with his heart.

***

With the situation worsening overseas, Corporal Richard Marak requested deployment and assignment to Iraq. Corporal Marak did not wait to be asked; he asked to serve because, in his heart, he knew it was the right thing to do and because he felt he was needed.

Jim Smith hosted a send-off party in the backyard of his home and it was filled with hundreds of lives that young Dick Marak has touched. At one point, Corporal Marak stood at attention, in his dress blues, and told the gathering of his pride for all of us and that he was choosing to go to Iraq to represent us, "You are my family."

When it was time to have that last conversation and say goodbye to Dick for a year of uncertainty and danger, I was grateful for the opportunity to remind him how immensely proud I was of him as a person, and to tell Corporal Richard Marak that he represents the best in all of us. He told me that serving where he is needed the most is something that he always wanted to do, and it is what he signed up for when he chose to become a Marine. "I want to go to Iraq and do the right thing. I want to help." I asked him not to forget the kids and Dick smiled and said, "I'm bringing chocolate for the kids. I want to help them there, and I can't wait to get back here because there is so much more I want to do to help Dreams for Kids."

While serving his tour Dick was promoted and returned as Sgt. Richard Marak. Dick kept his promise and remembered the kids in Iraq. He regularly visited them in the streets, gave them gifts and encouragement, and lived up to his extraordinary character.

Dick Marak is twenty-nine years-old. To me, he is part brother, part son, part friend, and all hero. To the world he is a gift and a living example of how character is defined by the strength of one's heart and the example of one's actions.

With Dick Marak and Jim Smith showing us how it was done, our organization's resolve became stronger to find others who had been lost in the isolation of disability. As we began our travels with J.J., we discovered an entire society of children waiting to be found.

14

Would You—
Michael Jordan—
Be My Valentine?

You will find as you look back upon your life that the moments when you have truly lived are the moments when you have done things in the spirit of love.

~ Henry Drummond

As the summer of 1997 turned to fall, J.J. invited me to RIC, the Rehabilitation Institute of Chicago, which has a 4,000 square foot facility specially created for persons with disabilities, The RIC Helen M. Galvin Center for Health and Fitness.

J.J. was waiting at the front, and as we entered the building it was readily apparent that this was no ordinary facility. The busy traffic of people who we make little notice of at most public facilities is vastly different at this facility. This is because the majority of people in this building lobby and elevators are in wheelchairs, or use crutches or walkers.

The Galvin Center, a workout facility for those with

disabilities, was made possible by a generous gift from the Galvin family and a grant from the Chicago Blackhawk Charities and the McCormick Tribune Foundation and is an extraordinary contribution to the community. J.J. told me, "There are not many facilities like this for people like me. A place where I can be active and workout, just like everyone else, like I used to before I was injured."

Looking around, it is fascinating to see a complete range of cardiovascular and full-body workout equipment, which appears to be no different than what you would expect to find in a large, private, fitness facility. However, upon closer examination, you discover that the equipment has been modified for wheelchairs to slide in as stationary seats rotate out. You also realize that the exercise machines, which allow you to work your chest, back, shoulders or arms, are otherwise the same as those machines, which are not accessible for those with disabilities. My initial thought was to wonder why you do not see these modified machines at the large, private, fitness facilities, especially when I found out that the cost of these machines are almost the same as the standard ones. It would be my first of many lessons on accessibility for those with disabilities.

While the attendant on the exercise mat was stretching J.J.'s limbs, it was my first glimpse into the condition that he lives with every single day. J.J. has been able to carry himself in such a way that you forget that he has a disability, and you simply see him. However, seeing him lying on the mat and being assisted, his disability became startlingly obvious. You see that if someone does not move his leg, it will not move at all. Lying down, his entire body is completely motionless. You are clearly reminded that J.J. is paralyzed.

One day, many years later, J.J. confided in me that the toughest time for him is the early morning, since he is a morning person. He gets up with the sun and is ready for the day. The problem is that no one else in the house is up that early. So he waits. The reality of the wait is the harsh reality of his paralysis.

If no one comes, he will never move. J.J. says, "The best I can describe it, is that it feels like being locked in a trunk, every day, and that you are waiting until someone finds you. You just hope that they do."

Although it has been many years since that day, and though we have become good friends and have spent much time together, I remember that day at RIC like it was yesterday. I was kneeling on the exercise mat, trying to come to terms with my racing thoughts as J.J. was just lying there, completely motionless, except for a single limb being moved by someone else. Yet he looked up and smiled, and he asked questions about me. It was as if we were sitting on a park bench, talking about the Cubs.

That is J.J.'s gift. It is a gift that served as a vehicle to bring light to an entire community, and inspired Dreams for Kids to be part of the solution.

The reality is that J.J., and all those living with a disability, truly need the rest of us. Just a little help, just some equal access and then they can be themselves and live their lives as who they are and the person they have always wanted to be.

To be available to give that help reminds me of the code Jesse White lives by, "No one has gotten to where they are without the help of others. That is why we are required to help the next person." Whether it is poverty, or any other disability, more help for them is needed.

As I marveled at this active workout facility and all which was done to help bridge that gap, J.J. practiced a little mind reading as he broke my thoughts and said, "Don't be fooled by all of this. This is a great place, but I am one of the lucky ones. There are so many people who do not have all of this."

The next time we met, I took J.J. to the place where I worked out, one of those big, expansive facilities that do not have seats which rotate out. There was not much for him to do there. At this place, full of able-bodied people going about their business of working out, I became very much aware of the stares. Soon the mood changed, and it became one of those, "Take me out of the pool so I won't ruin it for anyone else" moments. Without a trainer in sight, and a shortage of dolphins to save the day, we decided, instead, to have lunch.

Soon J.J. introduced me to another facility that he said was filled with kids like him, but those kids were the "unlucky ones." "These kids are poor, on top of everything else, and many have been abandoned by their own families. If there are kids that really need someone, it is these kids," J.J. explained. "If I had a million dollars, I would give it all to help those kids. It seems like everyone has forgotten about them."

Carmen's Friend

The Illinois Center for Rehabilitation and Education (ICRE) is a State of Illinois run facility, which offers continuing education and social services to underprivileged children with disabilities. ICRE is constantly on the brink of being closed due to lack of funding as well as government budget cuts; a prospect that is unthinkable for its many residents.

If ICRE closed, most of its residents would have nowhere to go. Nursing homes would be the last resort, which is the end of the line. The residents of ICRE are as young as four-years-old.

Carmen Villafane has been associated with ICRE for most of her life. She is a tireless volunteer, administrator and social worker. Carmen has worked with the staff and residents of ICRE with a passion and commitment to keeping ICRE operating and available to serve children who have few voices left that speak on their behalf.

What makes Carmen's continued service to ICRE all the more remarkable is that she was born with severe cerebral palsy, and has been in a wheelchair since she was a baby. She has undergone over thirty-five operations in her young life. Carmen has lived the pain of being excluded and feels the pain of the residents of ICRE.

Carmen, like most of us in Chicago and around the world, was a big Chicago Bulls' fan, and in particular, an even bigger Michael Jordan fan. Getting a ticket for a Bulls' game in the 1990's was about as easy as getting an audience with the Pope. In the late 1980's the prospects were more realistic, but it was still very difficult to obtain a ticket. So she was content to watch every single game on television.

However, Carmen's parents were determined to get her a ticket inside the Chicago Stadium, where the legend was being created and inside the arena that held the object of their daughter's affection. They saved and found a way to give her the surprise of her life. Carmen would be going to a Bulls' game. In 1988 she was fifteen-years-old. After her parents delivered the exciting news that she was the proud holder of Bulls' tickets, she spent days making the perfect Valentine's Day card and dreamed of giving it to Michael Jordan.

Carmen arrived early on the day of the game, and well before the game began she was watching the Bulls practice. Her father dared her to give Michael her Valentine's Day card. Carmen was too nervous to say anything to Michael, so she asked a security guard if he would ask Michael to turn around.

To Carmen's surprise the security guard said yes, and to her even bigger surprise Michael did indeed turn around. Carmen's heart raced and she opened her mouth, but not a single word came out. Michael smiled and said, "Is that card for me?" as he walked over to accept it. Michael told her that he appreciated the card very much and then he returned to the court. She found out later that it was against the rules to bring anything to the players while they were on the court, and it was unheard of for any player to respond to a fan before the game, in particular Michael Jordan, whose focus and intensity were legendary.

Carmen returned to her seat smiling from ear to ear. She had actually met Michael Jordan and he had accepted her Valentine's Day card.

I Will Always be Your Valentine

Each friend represents a world in us, a world possibly not born until they arrive, and it is only by this meeting that a new world is born.

~ Anais Nin

Carmen returned home that night and told her family and friends that meeting Michael Jordan and having him accept her Valentine's Day card was the thrill of her life and one she would never forget.

As the Bulls' season progressed, Carmen became even more emotionally invested in the games as she watched them on television. She would cheer for Michael Jordan like the rest of us, but unlike most of us, she had met Michael and had even given him a card. Carmen was beaming with pride as she told her friends.

One day, Carmen was visiting the Auto Show at the enormous 1.6 million square foot McCormick Place Convention Center on Chicago's lakefront. To her amazement, Michael Jordan was up on stage speaking to the crowd, in his capacity as a spokesperson for Chevrolet. Carmen asked an usher if she could move her wheelchair near the front, close to the stage.

Carmen raised her hand to ask Jordan a question but was so nervous that the woman next to her had to ask for her, "Do you remember her?" Michael answered with a smile, "Sure, I do. She gave me that nice Valentine's card." Then he asked Carmen why she had missed so many games. She remembers being so stunned that Jordan actually remembered her, that she was unable to speak. "I went home and was not able to speak for the rest of the day and night. I just could not believe that Michael Jordan remembered me," Carmen recalls.

About a month later Carmen's parents were able to purchase another set of tickets for her to attend another game. Carmen arrived early and located her seat in the area reserved for those with disabilities. As soon as she settled in, she looked up and standing right in front of her was # 23. Michael Jordan smiled and then asked with a serious look, "Where have you been? I've been looking all over for you."

Carmen was shocked, but realized that, this time, she better say something or Michael would think she could not talk at all. "I'm sorry. I didn't know you'd be looking for me. It is very hard for us to get tickets for the games." Michael replied, "Any time you want to come to a game, give me a call." He summoned a team manager who brought a pen and a piece of paper. Michael wrote down his phone number and handed it to Carmen.

Carmen waited a few days and called the phone number. The woman who answered said, "Michael said you would be calling. He has tickets waiting for you."

Carmen attended that game and a few others and asked to pay for the tickets. Jordan insisted that the tickets were a gift, but she felt badly about asking for so much and did not attend another game that year.

At the beginning of the Bulls' next season, Carmen received a special delivery at home. On the front of the package was the logo for the Chicago Bulls. Inside was a note and on it were the words: *I have missed you at the games. I can't wait to see you at the first game this year.* The note was signed, *your friend, Michael Jordan.*

Also inside were season tickets, and there would be season tickets for every year to follow.

When Carmen arrived at the first game, she was stunned. The usher led her to her soon to be regular seat. Her seat was right next to the last seat on the Bulls' bench.

As most basketball fans know, for the few minutes that Jordan took a break from the game, that last seat on the Bulls' bench was Michael's seat. In a few minutes time, as the crowd got fired up for the pre-game player introductions, Carmen Villafane was sitting right next to Michael Jordan.

From that first game, through all the winning seasons and six championships, to the final game at the end of his career with the Bulls, Carmen Villafane sat right next to Michael Jordan on the Bulls' team bench.

Carmen became one of the regular fixtures at the most exciting games in this town or in most any other town. It is fun to look at old pictures of those days, especially the pictures of Jordan, sitting on the bench, at the end of the fourth quarter, towel on his shoulders, ice packs on both knees. Sitting to Michael Jordan's right, with a big smile, is his good friend, Carmen Villafane.

Many seasons later, after one of his championships, Michael told Carmen he had something special for her. Jordan had won the Most Valuable Player Award in the NBA. Michael said he wanted her to have the ring. Carmen has worn it on a necklace around her neck ever since.

Even though Michael Jordan has long since retired, every single year he still sends Chicago Bulls' season tickets to Carmen. Even though she is sitting next to a different player these days, her favorite player is never far. Michael stays in touch with his friend Carmen, and she has Jordan's personal cell phone number, with an open invitation to call at anytime. "Michael is my friend," she says today.

Carmen moved into the award-winning Belden Apartments, the City of Chicago's first accessible apartment building; a facility built exclusively for adults who use wheelchairs. She also is happily married. Carmen met her husband, Chris, at ICRE. Until recently, she was working in computer technology at the Westside Veterans' Administration Hospital. Carmen is now a full-time Mom. Her beautiful daughter, Danielle, recently celebrated her 6th birthday.

The Door Opens a Little Wider

J.J. had introduced us to Carmen in 1998, and we invited her to our golf outing and welcomed her to Dreams for Kids. Carmen then invited me to ICRE, and I saw first-hand the faint glimmer of hope for children who had so little. I also experienced sadness for how truly little they had.

Carmen, like J.J, considers herself to be one of the "lucky ones." She still volunteers at ICRE and still gives her time and energy to keeping the doors of the facility open, in keeping the hope alive for the children who live and go to school at a place they call home. Carmen's friend, Michael, personally contributed $10,000 toward ICRE's programs. When the State of Illinois threatened to close the school, she helped organize a student protest at the State of Illinois building. That protest helped reverse the state's decision to close ICRE.

Our introduction to Carmen opened the doors for our organization to reach out to the children of ICRE. The kids of ICRE are included with our many guests at our Christmas party. Several of the children also participate in our summer programs, in activities that they had never before thought possible in their lives.

We fully invested in this new direction for Dreams for Kids, still remembering the traditions of our past, but adding children who had been isolated from much of what is taken for granted in everyday life.

We learned the lesson that Michael Jordan's friendship with Carmen transcends celebrity. Jordan's gesture and the integrity of his lasting friendship with Carmen were magnified by his status as a celebrity, but for those with disabilities, similar magic can also come from simple social interaction, with stares replaced by smiles and greetings.

In considering how our organization had reached this point, and in trying to make sense out of the fact that my personal exposure to the many people who are living with a disability had been so limited until J.J. dropped into my life, I was taken back in time to a fascinating play, whose role in my life did not become clear until years later.

The Boys Next Door

While attending DePaul University, I had been bitten by the acting bug. However, my dream of acting would be deferred until a later date. After graduation from law school, I spent six years establishing my law practice, and then, in 1988, one year before starting Dreams for Kids, I left the practice for an entire year to pursue acting full-time. It was a great choice and a year full of discovery.

After acting in several plays and doing the standard commercials and bit parts in television and film, I was chosen for a part in a play, which would affect me greatly. So much so that a group of friends and I decided to produce the play ourselves. The play, *The Boys Next Door*, directed by Ed Flynn, was written by Tom Griffin, and had performed on Broadway in 1988.

The play centers on a few days in the lives of four adults with various levels of developmental and physical disabilities, all living together in an apartment which served as state funded transitional housing. I came to learn that the program was remarkably similar to the facility that the state offers children in ICRE.

I played the part of Jack, "an overworked and underpaid social worker," whose job was to check up on the residents and to help them learn to integrate into independent living.

This is a powerful production since it gives you a glimpse into the lives of those who live with disabilities, as well as giving you the very best of theatre; an opportunity to laugh, cry, and to go home thinking.

The play followed the men throughout their daily lives, allowing the audience to witness their struggles, and their triumphs. Uncomfortable at first, not knowing how to respond, the audience soon allowed itself to laugh with the characters and to experience life as they lived it.

Unique to any other play was that, at various times during the production, the stage lighting shifted, giving each of the men their opportunity to slowly face the audience as they left their disability behind. In that moment, the men told the audience what it was really like to be "disabled," and how it felt to be viewed that way by others. These were very powerful moments. My character had several opportunities to explain to the audience the frustrations of the character's lives, as well as his own.

The character who had the most significant physical and developmental disability was a man by the name of Lucien. An all too real, insensitive, and out of touch moment, mirroring the State of Illinois' attempt to close ICRE occurred in our play. The state where this apartment was located was considering withdrawing funding for Lucien's transitional apartment. The government's decision would send the men to a group home, much the same as the nursing homes where the children of ICRE would have been sent.

To top it off, the state's department responsible for this decision had decided to hold hearings, and the resident they chose to testify was Lucien, the resident who had the most difficulty communicating.

It was my character, Jack's, responsibility to prepare Lucien for this hearing. This was an impossible task, and it made for a painful statement on government bureaucracy and the decisions that may come from that bureaucracy. Lucien was nervous beyond reach and he settled on the fact that wearing a Spiderman tie and reciting the alphabet was all he needed to impress the committee.

On the appointed day, Lucien, Spiderman tie and all, struggled mightily to speak, and as I put my arm around him the stage lights mercifully dimmed. Then a single spotlight lit center stage. There was Lucien, standing with head bowed.

In what I have always felt to be one of the great theatrical moments, Lucien's head slowly rose to face the audience, and at the same time his arm slowly straightened and his stooped posture became military straight. After a pause, Lucien spoke to the audience in a clear and strong voice.

I stand before you a middle-aged man in an uncomfortable suit, a man whose capacity for rational thought is somewhere between a five-year-old and an oyster. I am retarded. I am damaged. I am sick inside from so many years of confusion, utter and profound confusion. I am mystified by faucets and radios and elevators and newspapers and popular songs. I cannot always remember the names of my parents. But I will not go away. And I will not wither because the cage is too small. I am here to remind the species... of... the species. I am Lucien Percival Smith. And without me, without my shattered crippled brain, you will never again be frightened by what you might have become. Or indeed, by what your future might make you.

Over the next few years, I thought about this scene many times, yet never once did I realize the role it would one day play in my life.

Lucien and all those like him may be reminders of what the future might hold for any of us, or indeed, what might have been. However, I have come to learn there is so much more to it.

Lucien is more than a reminder. He is a person. One who interacts differently than many of us, but interacts nevertheless. To see past the obvious differences, and reach past the obvious fears that existed within me, for lack of knowledge, was to be my challenge.

J.J. and Carmen shed light on those fears, and this knowledge brought to light a whole new understanding of those who live with a disability.

What was surprising to me was the simplicity of bridging the divide that existed between us. It was as simple as embracing the reality of one of J.J.'s favorite statements, which is, "I am the same as you, just sitting down." Then he adds with a smile, "But don't make me get up!"

The focus of Dreams for Kids had shifted as seamless as the lights which faded on that theatre stage. When the spotlight was returned to center stage, our organization had begun to serve as a vehicle for all people to follow the lead of Carmen's friend, and "Be like Mike."

We now work to create opportunities to bridge the gap between able-bodied children and adults, and those children living with a disability. In that work, we discovered the magnificence of the dolphin that exists in all of us, and be witness to the extraordinary life changing effects that come from that discovery.

Michael Jordan accepted Carmen's Valentine and would hold her friendship and love for a lifetime. Dick Marak's mature vision allowed him to see right past J.J.'s wheelchair and accept a new friend in his life, with all of his heart. Dreams for Kids embraced these examples and realized the pure magic of it all begins with a simple hello.

15

See Past the Chair and Just Say "Hi"

I shall pass through this world but once. Any good therefore that I can do or any kindness that I can show to any human being, let me do it now. Let me not defer or neglect it, for I shall not pass this way again.

~ Mahatma Gandhi

There are an estimated 54 million people in the United States living with some form of disability. The disabled community is the largest minority group in the country. The numbers add up to nearly 1 out of 5 people. Of this number, nearly 8 million are children living with developmental and/or physical disabilities. According to the United Nations, ten percent of the world's population has a disability, over 600 million people.

The lives of children living with disabilities can include intense mental, emotional, and physical challenges. These children generally have little access to opportunities routinely enjoyed by other children. The saddest fact of all is that the majority of children living with a disability feel a pronounced sense of isolation.

This isolation is not limited to the inevitable confinement to their home. As we discovered, being treated differently is the act that creates the divide between those with disabilities and those who are able-bodied.

We found that, for those with disabilities, it is the little things that make up the day and add up to quality of life. Often times it is as simple as being recognized. It may be as easy as just saying "Hi."

Just Say Hi!

Never underestimate the power of your actions. With one small gesture you can change a person's life. For better or worse. God puts us all in each other's lives to impact one another in some way.

~ Jane Wagner

Gus Zografopoulos lost both of his legs in a car accident when he was still a young man. Nevertheless, he has adapted to his life as a double amputee with enthusiasm, boundless energy and a great sense of humor. Gus is able to drive a car, live independently, work, and pursue activities in a way that would make most able-bodied people envious.

Gus is a great friend of Dreams for Kids. Aside from being the best chef this side of Athens, he is also Head Coach of our local Power Soccer teams. Power Soccer is a wheelchair sport designed by two Canadian athletes. The game is played much the same way that soccer is played, but with motorized wheelchairs. Each motorized wheelchair is equipped with a molded surface on the front, which aids in striking the ball and pushing it down the court.

Gus has spent a considerable amount of time helping others adapt to living with a disability and has also concentrated on bridging the divide that exists between the disabled and the able-bodied community in which he was once a resident. A few years ago, he designed a button that says, *Just Say "Hi."* This simple greeting is where it can all begin but with alarming regularity never does for those with disabilities.

What Gus knows well, is that without the magic of Dick Marak's intervention and the convenience of a dance floor to pull it off, every day social interactions can be the most difficult of challenges for those with disabilities, especially for those using a wheelchair.

After I met J.J., we went to a restaurant for the first time. I pushed his wheelchair toward the restaurant door wondering how I was going to maneuver opening the door and pushing the chair through the door at the same time. Just then someone stepped in front of us, opened the door and walked inside, letting the door slam on the front of the wheelchair. As my mouth fell open in disbelief, J.J. looked back at me, smiled, and said, "Welcome to my world." He then nonchalantly added, "That kind of thing happens all the time."

This was a startling introduction into the way people in wheelchairs can be just ignored as if they were not even present. Many times I have had people talk to me while completely ignoring J.J. Some people even have asked questions about J.J., ignoring the fact that he is sitting right there.

It is the sum total of a day's worth of experiences like this that can add up to a heart wrenching feeling of being left out. It seems the younger the person is, the more he or she is ignored.

Our organization has found that it is in small steps that great progress can be made in lessening the distance between those with disabilities and those who are able-bodied. The impact of simple recognition can be much more than a person ever anticipates.

Catching the Right Elevator

The golden moments in the stream of life rush past us,
and we see nothing but sand; the angels come to visit
us, and we only know them when they are gone.

~ George Eliot

It seems that an elevator can sometimes take us to more than just our own floor.

Several years ago, I told a story to the guests of our annual golf outing dinner. The story involved an experience I had at a football game the weekend prior to that dinner.

I attended the football game as a guest of a young man whom I was mentoring at the time and who was playing for the home team. At halftime, as I was walking to the parking lot and in the middle of the only entrance or exit from the football stadium, there sat a young man in a motorized wheelchair. As I walked past him, I smiled and said Hi. In response, the young man, whose name, ironically, was J.J., said, "Can you help me? My chair is stuck in the mud." I told him that sure I could help and in a couple of seconds we were in the parking lot. As he thanked me with much more gratitude than I deserved, I asked him how long he had been sitting there. He replied, "I don't know, about ten minutes."

I asked him why he had not asked someone else to help in all that time and he replied that most people do not talk to him or even make eye contact, so it is hard to get their attention. "You said hello to me and you smiled."

It has been years since that football game, but it is still fresh in my mind. This kid was a junior at the very same college, was stuck in a hole in the middle of the only way in or out of the football stadium, for ten minutes, and not one of the hundreds of students or adults passing him said a single word to him or even looked in his direction.

As it turns out, I was the guest of the Booster Club that

day and they were hosting a barbecue. I asked J.J. if he was hungry, and in that all too familiar refrain heard from most college students he said, "I'm always hungry!" As he worked his way through his second burger he held court with the majority of the Booster Club and I was struck by how engaged they were, and how much everyone enjoyed themselves in his company. It reminded me that all we really need are more opportunities together, to enable us to break down the walls and to reach out to those who are different from us.

As I finished telling this story to our guests that evening, I then told them about Gus' *Just Say "Hi"* pin, which I was wearing at the time.

The following year, at the next golf outing dinner, a woman approached me and smiled. She then told me that she had been embarrassed as she listened to the story I had shared the year before. Now, it seemed that this woman had a story of her own to tell.

"There is a woman who lives in the same apartment building as I do and, two or three days a week, we have been in the elevator at the same time. This woman is in a wheelchair, and even though I would see her in the elevator several times a week, not once did I say hello. I may have smiled once or twice, but most often I just looked up at the numbers or down at the floor."

"I felt so ashamed that night when I heard your story and I made a commitment to change. The very next time I saw this woman I would look her in the eye, smile and say hello. The next morning the elevator doors opened on the sixteenth floor and there she was. When I said Hi and smiled, we immediately struck up a conversation and found out that we had a lot in common." After a hesitation, she wiped away a tear and said, "We have been great friends ever since."

I love that story. Every day, month after month, there was a friend waiting for her in that elevator. All it took to find her was a single word. *Hi.*

"I'm Not a Kid Anymore"

*How can I be useful, of what service can I be? There is
something inside of me, what can it be?*
~ Vincent Van Gogh

When J.J. turned twenty-one, he approached me and said,
"I am not a kid anymore. I cannot accept Dreams for Kids'
generosity any longer. I want to help kids. I would like to help
Dreams for Kids help others the way you have helped me."

I thought about that for a second, and as I have been known
to do gave J.J. more than he bargained for. I told him, "There
is an opening on the Dreams for Kids' Board of Directors and
I am going to nominate you for that position." I think he had
initially planned on first putting his toes in the water, but I told
him, "What the heck jump right in, the water's warm."

At first, J.J. felt he was not ready for the responsibility of
being a Director on the Board. However, after the Board took less
time to vote him in than it did to nominate him, he reconsidered
and became a member of the Board of Directors of Dreams for
Kids. In the idealized way that I tend to view things, there could
not have been a better person as our first Board member with a
disability than the one who had been the beacon of light that lit
our path to an expanded awareness of the disabled community.

Shortly after J.J.'s swearing in and requisite hazing, it was
time to go to work. We had been told of a young boy named
Alex who was losing his battle against a rare blood disorder. His
family was struggling mightily to keep it together emotionally
and financially. The boy's father was saving money to purchase
tickets to a Chicago Bears' game so that his son, for the first time,
could see his favorite team, the Green Bay Packers. The game
was sold out and tickets were next to impossible to obtain.

Fortunately, things have a way of working out in Chicago.
We "got a guy," as we say, and that guy happened to work in the
front office of the Bears. The Chicago Bears have always been

great to the community and have been a great friend to Dreams for Kids. One phone call and we had tickets for Alex and his dad, on the 50-yard line, no less, Green Bay side, directly behind their bench. The Bears even ensured that Alex's favorite player, Brett Favre, provided Alex with a #4 Green Bay jersey to wear to the game.

It was J.J.'s job to deliver the tickets to Alex. When Alex's mother opened the door and saw J.J. with the tickets in his lap, she dropped to her knees, hugged him and cried. She said that since Alex found out that he was going to the game with his dad, he had not been able to sleep from the excitement. She said Alex had not been this happy for a long time.

So that Sunday, sitting in the best seats in the house, were a little boy and his dad, cheese wedges on their heads, spending a day together in a dream come true.

The Circle of Giving

The greatest virtues are those which are most useful to other persons.

~ Aristotle

In 1997, when we reached out to J.J. O'Connor we did so not because of his disability, but rather because of how he chose to reach past his own loss and use his ability to help someone else in need.

J.J. was someone with a disability, but was also someone who embraced the great value of reaching out to others. In our work with Dreams for Kids, we have found that most people have the desire to make a difference. The challenge for many is finding the right opportunity to be involved. It has been our mission, not just to do what we can to assist children, but to also open the door wide enough for others to have an opportunity to be involved.

The lives of our volunteers and their families have been impacted greatly. Time and time again people have told us how much participating as a volunteer has done for *them*.

There is one school of thought, which certainly is part of the Jesse White School, that none of us has gotten to where we are without the help of others. Therefore, we have an obligation to help the next person.

While I am a graduate and card-carrying member of Jesse's School, reaching out to others has also proven to be its own reward.

Time and time again, volunteers have returned from a day of doing something positive for others filled with a special kind of gratitude. It is the type of gratitude that goes far beyond the realization of how fortunate we are for not having a disability or for not being underprivileged. It is a deeper realization that we have made a difference which transcends our own personal world. We have done something to enhance the quality of life in our time, as well as for future generations. This is the true reward and it elevates one's life in ways that are immeasurable.

I have gratefully discovered that one of the substantial benefits from working with our organization is that I have had the good fortune to meet so many people who enjoy such a high quality of life. In my other career, as an attorney, I have seen many individuals who have reached great financial success. Yet I have only seen true happiness in those who have also been of service to others.

Just the other day, in the early morning, I spoke to Jesse White as he sat in a car, in the parking lot of a grade school, preparing to speak to a class of children. Later that day, I had dinner with Jim Smith, as Jim waited for J.J., who was spending time with a group of younger people whom he had just met. Both men were fulfilling responsibilities that consumed a significant part of their lives and for which each is well known.

On that day it occurred to me that these two men are two of the happiest and most fulfilled people whom I have ever known.

Both have realized significant success in their chosen careers, yet in all that they do, they are always grounded in service to others.

These two individuals have taken service to others to a level that many people have assumed has taken away from their own personal lives. The reality is that their service has not taken them from their family or friends, but rather, has added an enormous value to their lives. Jim told me that evening, "Many people ask why I have made this commitment to J.J. and question how much it has taken away from me. However, just the opposite is true. I wake up every single day so happy for the life that I have chosen."

That from small acts of kindness, to hours spent in volunteering, all the way to an entire lifetime of dedication to others, with each increase in service to another person, there is a greater increase in personal fulfillment in return.

A Life of Ability

> *Begin each day to live and count each day as a separate life.*
>
> ~ Seneca

J.J. O'Connor has called October 24th 1995, "the best day of my life." October 24th 1995, is the day J.J. broke his neck.

I have listened to him say this many times, and each time he says it, his conviction becomes stronger. It is as if he sensed it to be true when he was younger and has become more and more convinced of its truth as his life has unfolded.

"I would never have received all the love and support from so many people if I had not gotten injured. I would never have had all the experiences which I have had."

"I have found that many people who become disabled spend a lot of time thinking of the life they would have had if not for their injury. I realize that I am the person I am today because of my injury."

J.J. said this to me a short time ago. He went on to say, "It is really what you do with your life that counts. I have seen more paralysis among able-bodied people."

Not giving into perceived limitations and seeking to excel with all the gifts he had been given, J.J. completed his studies at Lake Forest College, earned a Bachelors in Business Administration and did so in such a manner that he was chosen to represent his class at graduation. Good Morning America covered his class commencement address and broadcast it to the entire nation. When it was time for the President of Lake Forest College to congratulate him, J.J., with Jim Smith at his side to support him, stood from his wheelchair, tall and proud, and received his diploma.

Upon graduation, J.J. committed himself to reaching others in any way he was able and became an inspirational public speaker.

Being a part of J.J.'s life of extraordinary ability was further motivation for Dreams for Kids to expand its mission for children with disabilities. J.J.'s full life and continued desire to give back to others in need fueled our desire to find opportunities for others to be able to do the same.

In the year 2000, in one of our meetings, the Board was discussing ways which it could address the most difficult of situations, namely the quality of life in both of the groups whom we represent—those with disabilities and those with financial challenges. We had long since recognized and responded to the disability of poverty and had come to understand and assist those with physical or developmental disabilities. However, to recognize the intense isolation of those who had a combination of these disabilities was shocking.

Those who live in poverty and have other disabilities are part of a lost society. With no means to gain even a limited access to everyday life that can be available for a person with disability, those who are also underprivileged can be confined to a barely accessible home. Some underprivileged children living with a disability, particularly those whose disability was the result of an injury, are limited to one or two rooms in their house. Some have never even had a meal with their family in their own kitchen. To travel outside the home is often impossible without the aid of a specialized vehicle, which most of the time is non-existent.

In our Board meeting, we made a decision to expand our programming that resulted in benefits we could never have imagined, and for which we will forever be grateful.

It is no surprise that the person who opened the door to this future was Jim Smith. After J.J. discussed the overwhelming needs for students at ICRE and all those in similar situations, Jim said, "There are so many kids for whom, once the school year is over, never leave their homes. There are no busses to pick them up, nor do their families have an accessible van. These kids might never leave their homes all summer. There has to be a way that we can provide some recreation for them."

When J.J. suggested that we contact RIC to explore the possibility, we had a feeling that this was going to be something special. Not in a million years could we have known just how special this effort would prove to be. We were about to set sail on a course that would level the playing field for children with disabilities and have an astonishing effect on the kids and their families' quality of life.

As I prepared to contact RIC, my thoughts drifted back to my graduation year from college. In 1979, Chicago was graced by the visit of a truly extraordinary dolphin. This individual touched the world in the most special of ways, and he left an unprecedented legacy of compassion and faith. I decided to contact a man whose life was blessed in amazing ways by this remarkable Shepherd, and it was this man's example that we used to launch the dreams of children who awaited blessings of their own.

16

Blessed by the Pope

Every encounter we have, even if brief and seemingly unimportant, may have more significance than we know. A brief encounter may begin a greater ripple that reaches its intended purpose years later. Everyone who comes into our lives may be part of our mission, and we, a part of theirs. Understanding this can give meaning to the common events of life. By being positive and helpful toward others, even in casual moments, we can make the most of our time on earth.

~ The Ripple Effect

In October of 1979, Pope John Paul II visited Chicago and held mass in Soldier Field. When any Pope travels, it is always a near-historic event. However, Pope John Paul II's presence touched people in a very special way. Illinois has a significant Polish population, and Chicago has the largest Polish contingent outside of the Polish capital of Warsaw. The Polish community was swept up in the excitement of this once in a lifetime event and was joined by worshippers of all faiths who came by the tens of thousands to see the Pope.

Blessing for a Lifetime

In January of that same year, a nine-year-old boy contracted a rare blood disease called meningococcemia, one of the rarest forms of meningitis. As a result of his illness, all four of his limbs had been amputated.

On a windy and cold October day, on the streets of Chicago near Holy Name Cathedral, amidst a huge crowd, that same boy, Bobby Lujano, sat in a wheelchair next to his grandmother, as they waited for the Pope. His grandmothers name was Hope.

Bobby's grandmother, a devout Catholic, had done everything she could for her youngest grandson, including taking him to the Rehabilitation Institute of Chicago in August 1979, for therapy. Hope brought Bobby to Holy Name Cathedral that day praying that the Pope would bless him, and that the Pontiff's blessing would give Bobby hope. The enormous crowd of people standing in line, however, stretched out for miles. Police estimated that over 200,000 people waited, with only a handful able to enter the Cathedral.

A Chicago policeman on duty that day, Jim Zwit, saw Bobby and his grandmother huddled on the sidewalk as he was walking in the street. There were many people on this Chicago street, but Officer Zwit was drawn to Bobby and Hope. He stopped to ask them if there was anything he could get for them. Bobby was cold so Jim Zwit got him some hot chocolate and covered him with a blanket. Officer Zwit then decided he would wait with Bobby and his grandmother and for the next seven hours that is just what he did, as they inched toward the Cathedral.

As time passed, it became clear that there was no chance at all that Bobby and his grandmother would make it inside the Cathedral. Faced with the disappointment of a boy who had suffered so much and a grandmother who had brought him so far, Officer Zwit made a decision. He would do whatever it would take to make sure that the Pope saw Bobby.

Officer Zwit directed Bobby and his grandmother to follow

him past the long line. He took Bobby's wheelchair around the police lines, inside the Cathedral, and figured that, if he had gotten this far he might as well go the distance. Officer Zwit continued down the aisle of the Cathedral, straight to the front and right next to velvet rope, directly in front of the stairs where the Pope was to enter.

"I decided that any trouble I would get into for bringing this boy inside the police lines was well worth it." Zwit recalled. "I would do what it would take to see if we could get some sort of audience with the Pope."

As Bob Lujano now recalls, "When the Pope first appeared in Holy Name Cathedral, I will never forget the chills that I felt when I saw him and how radiant he looked. I had never seen another person glow or illuminate like he did. He was surrounded by a very powerful aura, yet he stood subtle and peaceful."

As the Pope entered, he paused to bless the crowd and as he turned to his right, he saw young Bobby and walked toward him. As Bobby looked up, the Pope placed his hands on Bobby's face, and offered a special blessing in Latin. The Pope then gave him his rosary. Bobby kissed the Pope's ring and then looked directly into the Pontiff's eyes. Later he said, "I was left feeling inspired, joyous, exhilarated, and overwhelmed with the feeling that I had been in the presence of a very special man."

It was at that very moment that Bobby was filled with a feeling that his grandmother was so desperately seeking for him. Young Bobby Lujano, for the first time since losing all four of his limbs and all thought of a future of any value, was filled with hope.

"I will always feel that my meeting with the Pope was the Will of God and a miracle in a sense. I was one of 200,000 people, and I got to meet him and receive his blessing and his rosary. It was the beginning of a new life, a different life, and a long rehabilitation process. It was about finding my purpose in life as a quadruple amputee. It was also the realization that everything was going to be alright. It was about God telling me, through the Pope, that He was with me. He was not going to let me fail."

"I knew then that I could go to school again, my family would be there for me, and my life could have meaning."

Divine Opportunities

Reaching even just one soul with the message of God's love sets into motion a reaction which passes that hopeful message to others and then to more, rippling out to reach countless souls.

~ The Awakening Heart

Bobby returned to high school having lost so much, yet having gained, by the intervention of a stranger, a blessing of spiritual inspiration, which would set the course and direction for his future. He dedicated himself to school with a renewed purpose.

After completing his studies and graduating from high school, Bobby was accepted into the University of Texas at Arlington where he excelled. He went on to graduate with a Bachelors of Administration in Pre-Law. He continued his education at the University of Tennessee and earned a Masters Degree in Sports Management.

Like most nine-year-old boys, Bobby had a love of sports. His love and desire to participate in those sports were not taken away when he lost his arms and legs.

He was an athlete before his injury and he was determined to prove he was still an athlete. All he needed was an opportunity. When he heard the words Quad Rugby, Bob knew the door was open and the competitor in him was ready for more than just participation.

Quad Rugby was developed by three Canadians as a quadriplegic alternative to wheelchair basketball. The sport was originally called Murderball because of the aggressive nature of the game. It was introduced to the United States by the University of North Dakota's Disabled Student Services who formed the first team and changed the name from Murderball to Quad Rugby.

Bob Lujano did not just play Quad Rugby; he became a champion. In ten years of playing Quad Rugby, he has won five U.S. Quad Rugby National Championships and was awarded an additional three medals playing Quad Rugby for Team USA, including the Gold Medal in the 1999 World Wheelchair Games.

Bob's achievements on the rugby field carried over to a career off the field that has been dedicated to helping other children realize their dreams. He has kept the circle of giving unbroken by reaching back to help and inspire other kids. His passion is giving other children with disabilities hope that their lives can have meaning.

For the past eight years, he has served as Coordinator of Athletics at the Lakeshore Foundation, an official U.S. Olympic and Paralympics Training Site. At Lakeshore, he works with young people with disabilities between the ages of five and twenty-one, providing them with recreational activities and instilling in them the skills to be both physically fit and to succeed in life. "We set a high level of expectation for them," Bob says. We want them to see themselves going to school, graduating, having a job and a full life for themselves, using everything God has given them."

When asked how he overcomes the challenges that come with his disabilities, he has a motto in life: "No arms, no legs, no problem!"

A few years ago, Bob had a featured role in the acclaimed movie on Quad Rugby, *Murderball*. You may not have heard of the movie. Much like the day to day existence of those with disabilities, the movie's release was isolated and limited. This was unfortunate since it has been universally hailed as one of the best documentaries in years. In film critic Roger Ebert's respected opinion, "...*Murderball* works like many great documentaries to transcend its subject and consider the human condition. We may not be in chairs and may not be athletes, but we all have disabilities, sometimes of the spirit. To consider the bleak months and sleepless nights when these men first confronted the reality of their injuries, and now to see them in the full force of athletic exuberance, is to learn something valuable about the human will."

On January 31, 2006, *Murderball* was nominated for an Academy Award for Best Documentary Feature of the Year.

Coming Home Again

The life I touch for good or ill, will touch another life and then in turn, another, until who knows when the trembling will stop or in what far place my touch will be felt.

~ Frederick Buechner

In April of 2005, Bob Lujano, was to play in the U.S. Quad Rugby Association Heartland Sectional in Chicago, Illinois. He used this opportunity to reunite with an old friend, retired Chicago Police Officer Jim Zwit. Bob and Jim Zwit had not seen each other since 1985. Their reunion would be bittersweet.

Although they had planned their reunion months prior, this weekend turned out to be one of worldwide mourning. As Bob and Jim embraced they did so with joy, but also with sadness, since the man who had inspired their meeting so many years ago was now dying. Pope John Paul II was nearing the end of his life after a long illness and the world was awaiting word of his death.

"I arrived in Chicago knowing that it was going to be an emotional weekend." Bob would recall. "I had plans to see family, to reunite with Jim, and to win a rugby tournament."

At 3:00 p.m. on Saturday, he learned that the Pope had passed away. He watched the reports on television and prepared to play the game that day in the Pope's honor. "It was definitely on my mind as I started to play," he recalled.

Playing with a purpose inspired by a great man's blessing that had changed his life; he played in honor of Pope John Paul II, in a city where his life had been born again.

With his inspired play, his team won that game and went on to win the national qualifying tournament. Bob was named the tournament's Most Valuable Player.

Later that evening, Bob visited Holy Name Cathedral where he had been blessed by the Pope so many years ago. "I will always remember that moment when I met him," he told me recently. "I had not known what purpose God had for me. Did He even have a purpose for me? What could I do? I had just lost my limbs. The moment was a spark, a springboard, a source of hope and inspiration. It was definitely something God had set up. I will always be thankful to God for His love, the Pope for his inspiration, Jim for his compassion, and to my family for their love and support."

"My life has gone beyond anything I could have ever imagined."

"The Pope left an indelible imprint on my mind, in my life, and he will be with me forever. As I speak to you today, I am looking at the picture of the Pope blessing me. It is on my desk. Whenever times are tough or I have a dark moment, I look at it and smile. I am reminded once more there is nothing that will prevent me from doing what I am supposed to do."

Above and Beyond the Call of Duty

Regret for the things we did can be tempered by time; it is
regret for the things we did not do that is inconsolable.

~ Sydney J. Harris

On that day in 1979, Chicago Police Officer Jim Zwit opened his eyes in the morning without any notion the day would be any different from any other day. He did not go on duty that day knowing that extraordinary circumstances were just hours away. As he walked down that sidewalk near Holy Name Cathedral, Officer Zwit might very well have walked past a young boy in a wheelchair and his grandmother. Jim Zwit's instincts told him otherwise.

When he chose to stop and say Hi and ask if he could be of assistance, doing so changed a life forever. It profoundly affected all those lives that Bob Lujano influenced in the future. This simple, yet gracious, choice also elevated Jim Zwit's life. He said his encounter with Bobby and the Pope blessed his own life in many ways.

"When I looked at that young boy twenty-five years ago, I really did not think he had a fair chance to be happy and succeed in life," Jim Zwit says now. "Boy, did he prove me wrong. They say in life that we are rewarded for the deeds we do. I certainly feel that I have been rewarded with being reunited with Bob this year. When I look at what he has accomplished so far in his life, I must say that perhaps Pope John Paul II started doing his miracles a long time ago."

The miracle of Bob Lujano's story and the significant role that sports played in his life served as inspiration to Dreams for Kids. We began working to extend his blessing to thousands of children with disabilities waiting for their own hope. Also waiting for us were entire families who never stopped believing in their children's dreams. It was time to remove the limitations, and offer them all a future of infinite possibilities.

It was time to say *"Hi...."*

17

A Pier Full of Empty Wheelchairs

It is in games that many men discover their paradise.
~ Robert Lynd

Recreational opportunities for children with disabilities are few and far between. For those children who also suffer the added disability of poverty, the opportunity to experience the sheer joy of participating in any sport is less than non-existent. Participation in sports, for them, exists only in their imaginations.

Children who have disabilities can be so far removed from the recreation, sport, and social activities that are routinely offered to able-bodied children that they retreat to their homes, with little hope of any meaningful participation. The closest most children with a disability come to sports is watching their able-bodied siblings from the sidelines.

Slowly and painfully, the seemingly endless activities that many able-bodied children take for granted become daily reminders of an improbable dream for a child with a disability.

Tom Richey was the Sports Director of the Rehabilitation Institute of Chicago. Since 1982, RIC Sports, through its Virginia Wadsworth Wirtz Sports Program, has been offering adults with disabilities, opportunities to participate in a wide variety of sporting and recreational activities, ranging from golf, softball and tennis to wheelchair basketball and Quad Rugby.

Until the year 2000, RIC Sports programs were limited to adults. When I called Tom Richey early that year to inquire about the possibility of expanding RIC's programming to include children with disabilities, he was amazed. Tom said, "We just scheduled a meeting to figure out a way to do just that! Would you like to come to our meeting next Wednesday?"

I certainly made time for that meeting. As is often the case when good intentions are put forth, good people show up to help make them happen. Tom Richey is one of those good people, and Tom and Dreams for Kids were a match made in paradise.

After a series of meetings, we wasted no time in initiating the Dreams for Kids' Summer Camp. In the summer of 2000, during our first year, we offered ten children with various forms of disabilities, the opportunity to play the sports of their dreams every Saturday. We called the pilot program, 'Super Summer Saturday Sports.' The next year, we dropped Saturday from the name as we added two additional days each week to the program. By the third year, in 2003, the demand for the program was overwhelming and the effect was everlasting.

We soon adopted the program and expanded it to include year round activities. We asked the kids to name it. They named it Extreme Recess. Not content with offering just the standard fare to children who had been denied access for a lifetime, we offered, in addition to gymnastics, baseball, softball, tennis, basketball and golf, activities as diverse as rock climbing, kayaking, martial arts, yoga, horseback riding, water skiing and sailing.

Each year we expanded our program to accommodate a growing waiting list of eager children anxious to find out if it was really possible to realize a dream they believed to be impossible.

In late 2006, the profound impact that the sports program was having on the children and their families increased our vision, and we began to see the necessity to reach out to as many children as possible. With great excitement and anticipation, we opened a national office in Washington DC, increased our programming across the United States, and into places in the world where children with disabilities are virtually hidden from society.

With the beginning of the eleventh year of our program, we are convinced of the importance of this effort, and that the sheer joy of being able to come from the sidelines of life and play sports literally changes lives.

Changing Lives...One Kid at a Time

Unless someone like you cares a whole, awful lot; things aren't going to get better, they're NOT!
~ Dr. Seuss, *The Lorax*

The lives that have been changed in the work we are fortunate to do are not just limited to the kids who participate in our programs. Parents, brothers, sisters and entire families have been affected in ways that give such enormous hope.

Volunteers have rediscovered the joys of childhood and the immeasurable value of giving that has carried over into their own lives and their families.

Sports can be viewed as a day's activity and as an opportunity for recreation. However, those who are denied participation in sports realize from afar the greater value in playing the games. There are friends to meet, places to go, and competition to expand one's confidence. Above all else, there is the essential feeling of belonging.

For a child to be part of something that previously they could only witness on television or from the sidelines, liberates them in a way that carries over into the rest of their lives.

Living with a disability can too often be thought of as living with a limitation. When children who have a disability are denied opportunities that are readily available to able-bodied children, this assumption can be reinforced. Once those obstacles are removed, the word limitation is to never return. The positive effect carries over to school and to their social lives. Roles are reversed in families that longed for that reversal and lives are never the same.

Anthony is a young boy who has cerebral palsy. Anthony's older, able-bodied brother is a high school soccer star. For his entire life Anthony has cheered his brother from the sidelines. There has never been a fan more enthusiastic or more loyal than Anthony. Sitting next to his parents, Anthony's cheers can be heard across the field, and probably down the block, every time his brother comes near the ball.

The introduction of Power Soccer became an open invitation for Anthony to come from the sidelines of life, and for his parents to do what they always dreamed of doing. It was also an opportunity for Anthony's brother to cheer for his hero.

In the winter of 2006, on a Wednesday night, in a Chicago indoor gymnasium, young Anthony was motoring his chair toward the ball with a smile from ear to ear. From the first row, cheering on their feet and from the bottom of their hearts, were the proudest parents and brother you could ever imagine watching a soccer game.

When we asked Anthony if he was having fun, he didn't have to smile, because that grin had never left his face from the moment he rolled onto the court. Anthony just looked straight up and said, *"Ohhh, my mom is going to be sooo proud of me!!"*

Fifteen Feet of Joy

Yes you can...but you ain't alone. I'm right here with ya. I've been here all along. Now play the game...your game. The one that only you was meant to play...The one that was given to you when you come into this world...You ready? Strike that ball Junuh...don't hold nothin' back. Give it everything...Now's the time. Let yourself remember... Remember YOUR swing.

~ The Legend of Bagger Vance

I love reading the Extreme Recess schedule. There is not a kid alive that would not be envious of the wide range of fun and challenging sports that fill the schedule. It is ever so sweet that the kids who are participating in our program are experiencing the very idea of sports for the first time. Now they can go back to school and be the envy of everyone. They can go from being the one left out, to hearing the words, "You are so lucky!"

One such sport is golf. At some point, most able-bodied kids have the opportunity to try their hand at this game, but for those with disabilities there is not much of a chance to tee it up. We offer golf instruction from volunteers, such as Patrick Byrne, who lost his leg as an adult and has dedicated his life to inspiring others with disabilities. Patrick could not drive a golf ball more than 40 yards after his injury. With an athlete's heart and dedication, he now reaches over 250 yards from the tee, while balancing on one leg! He even won the longest drive contest at our organizations annual golf outing.

However, the highlight for any golfer is not the driving range. It is getting out on the actual golf course.

Any golf course would be fine indeed for these kids, but if it is worth doing, it is worth overdoing. After all this *is* a dream summer. So our day on the links was at the private Merit Golf Club in Libertyville, Illinois, home to prestigious members, including a couple of guys named Tiger Woods and Michael Jordan.

The day begins like it does for any other golfer on the course—at the practice range, with a bucket of balls. However, the members and guests of the John Dolan Golf Challenge who share the range with us that day do not have it so lucky. We bring a PGA Pro or two for some last minute instructions.

After practice, it's time for a picnic lunch under the willow trees and then it's off to play the game. Our kids now have the opportunity to not just play on a golf course, but to play on the same course as Tiger Woods. I will never forget one year when Jonathan, who uses a walker that was his grandmother's, was pacing anxiously all through lunch, constantly asking, "Where's Tiger? Where's Tiger?"

It was time to line up on the first tee and in convenient sixteensomes; we were ready to play the course. One by one, each kid took his best swing on that tee, on the first hole of the Merit Golf Club. Many of the kids were in wheelchairs, some with braces, walkers or crutches, some missing an arm or a leg, or some had other visible disabilities. However, for that moment, every single one was a golfer.

I watched until the last golfer took his swing and then looked out across the fairway. There was not a single golf ball that landed more than fifteen feet from the tee. I will always remember looking next to the group of kids scrambling to their balls to set up their next shot. In a precious moment in time, it was as if all of their hardware had just disappeared. They were just like any other kid, filled with one unmistakable emotion—pure joy.

I have reflected on that scene often. When I do, I try to remember that no matter where I am, whether at work, at home, or playing a sport, when I take my very best shot—and it only goes fifteen feet—I look up and smile, joyful for simply having had the opportunity.

After a round of golf, it is time for the ceremony on the 19th Hole. Each golfer receives a Champion's Cup. There is a picture of Jonathan from our website, which sits on my desk at home. He is holding his Cup high above his head, with a look of pride that could match anyone who has ever worn the Green Jacket at the Masters.

As we were leaving for the day, Jonathan, holding his Cup under his arm while managing his oversized walker, stopped and put his head way back so he could see me from under the brim of his golf cap. With all seriousness, he said, "If you see Tiger—tell him I can golf!"

A Lake Touched by God

When we try to pick out anything by itself, we find it hitched to everything else in the Universe.

~ John Muir

The broad spectrum of sports our organization made available to children with disabilities continued to expand in our program. With its expansion came memories to last a lifetime, coupled with enough dreams to fill the future for a summer full of elated kids—and their parents.

One of the featured days of Extreme Recess is a water sports event held at Twin Lakes, Wisconsin. There is no finer example of a day that can transport one from the feeling of being left out, to being on top of the world.

There is a certain beauty to being on the water; or sitting on the shore or pier, just gazing at the waves of water. There is a beautiful mixture of action and serenity, as boats and water-craft intermittently speed past, only to leave the water calm once again, as the sun shines across the horizon, making it appear to stretch on forever.

There is great hope in just being near the water. It is said that water is where it all began, and where we shall return. The vast waters are also home to the dolphins. On this one day, in rural Wisconsin, the water is a place where dreams live.

We arrive with the rising of the sun, with a band of excited volunteers, and after a group breakfast we head to the pier to set up for the day. There is a canopy for us to set up over the length of the pier, water craft to line up, and two power ski boats to gas up and to get ready to launch. On the beach, lines of kayaks and floatable chairs wait in the sand at water's edge. The sound system needs fine-tuning and there are banners to be hung and flags to be raised. There is a half drum to fill for the barbecue lunch. Finally, after the life jackets and vests are hauled out, it is time to fill the parking lot with adaptive bikes and to mark off the obstacle course.

This is no ordinary day at the beach.

As we set the stage for this little corner of paradise and look out over the adaptive equipment, which now stretches from the parking lots to the beaches, and covers the pier and fills the water, we think of the nearly one hundred kids, with various disabilities, who are now at home, miles away. Soon they will be boarding a bus toward a day that has existed only in their imaginations.

Envision the uncommon scene of busload after busload of "disabled" children arriving at the beach. Now imagine a stream of those kids arriving there for the first time ever, flowing from the parking lot, eyes wide, smiles even wider, heading to the water, some with crutches, some on walkers, others in wheelchairs, some in braces and still others being carried by their parents or friends. There may be a better way to start a day, but I have a hard time thinking of what that would be.

Once the day officially begins, surrounded by serious organization, training and watchful supervision, it is a complete free for all—just what any kid would order.

On the beach and on the pier, the initial unbounded enthusiasm gives way to what is often seen when any kid experiences the unknown for the first time. "There is no way I am going on that!" "That" is this: Water craft rides, kayaking, riding a bicycle for the first time, floating in the water in a beach chair, or the highlight, being pulled behind a boat around the lake on water skis, at faster than bargained for speeds. One by one, each kid gathers the courage to try "that" and eventually all of "that," and cannot be pulled away.

After a traditional barbecue lunch, there is time to sit around and listen to the excited chatter of a happy bunch of kids. The second half of the day is more and more of the same. The grand finale is a water show presented by the famous Aquanut Water Show Team.

Of the many activities our organization has made possible, one that is particularly special is the magic of water skiing, now available for those with even the most severe disabilities. As we purchased pieces of equipment, one by one, the most prized piece is a simple, yet powerful piece of adaptive equipment; the outrigger ski and companion chair, one of several pieces of adaptive equipment contributed to the program by the engineering students of Northwestern University.

This adaptive equipment allows a child to be strapped into a chair, which is attached to two extra skis, one on each side of a single ski in the middle. The equipment is pulled by a special ski rope attached to the ski boat. Trained interns ride in watercraft alongside, as the boat speeds along the perimeter of the lake. We pull out the full guard of at least eight interns, riding two to a watercraft, when our resident quad, J.J. O'Connor, takes to the water, and of course, elects to drop the outriggers. This makes for some interesting moments, but the sight of J.J. sailing past the pier on his first fly by, arm raised, is one to truly treasure.

As kids witness others with disabilities take on such challenges, each is inspired to do more, and the result instills them with a confidence that carries over, not just for a day, but for the rest of their lives.

During one of our ski events, as I was walking to the parking lot, I saw an older man slowly walking with his hands in his pockets, appearing to be lost in thought. I waved as I approached him and he said hello. When I introduced myself, he said he was Chris's father, one of the kids in our camp. Chris is sixteen-years-old and was born with a severe neurological disorder. He has used a wheelchair his entire life.

Chris's father told me that he was on the way to call his wife and was trying to collect his thoughts. "This entire day has just been so overwhelming to me," he said. "My wife and I never imagined that our boy could play a sport, even though that is what he has always wanted to do. Now he has played all kinds of sports, all summer long, and today he is actually going to water ski." His voice broke as he struggled to control his emotions, "All of you must have been touched by God to have given my son so much happiness."

Later that same day, I sat down on the pier to collect my own thoughts, as another young man, Marcus, was being returned to his wheelchair after his third water skiing trip around the lake. With a towel on his shoulders and water dripping down his face, he looked out over the lake. The sun was beginning its descent, casting a glow on the water. Marcus quietly said, "This is really something." I replied that water skiing is really a great time. He looked at me in disbelief. "Water skiing? Man, I have never even seen a lake. I have never been on a pier. I didn't think that I would ever be on a boat. For kids like me, this is just unbelievable."

I could not resist asking him if this was a dream come true. I got what I deserved for fishing for the easy one—a dose of reality. "Dream? I would never have dared dream about something like this."

Another Day in Paradise

Forget yourself for others, and others will never forget you.

~ Author unknown

Over the past eleven years, I have witnessed Extreme Recess grow in ways which none of us could have ever imagined. It is not just in the increased number of children who now participate in the program that gives us such great hope. It is in the growth of the kids who have participated. It is also in the profound changes that have occurred in those who have reached out to these children. Every year, the program changes the lives of our volunteers, and changes my life.

Just a few months ago, at the beginning of our water sports day on the lake, I was telling a first-time volunteer about Chris and about meeting his father. I had not seen Chris for some time nor had I seen his father since that day. We were walking up the hill in Twin Lakes, toward the parking lot, and I suddenly stopped. I was standing at the exact same place where I had said hello to Chris's father years before. The emotion that came from that realization literally stopped me in my tracks. What was to happen next would remind me that there are greater forces at work in our lives, and it is in these moments that we realize that we are never alone.

As we stood on the place of that special meeting with Chris's dad, I had to take a moment to attempt to control my own emotions. As I looked up and toward the parking lot, I saw that the busses had arrived and the children were beginning to line up. I looked at our volunteer and looked back at the kids without being able to say a word. The first boy in line was Chris.

We walked up to meet the kids and when I said hello to Chris, he was attempting to say something to me. Chris's condition makes it very difficult for him to speak. I leaned in very close, and he said in a whisper, "I remember you."

One Special Day

There are no great things, only small things with great love. Happy are those.

~ Mother Teresa

Throughout the day, our newest volunteer was quiet, yet very engaged with the activities. At noon I asked her if she would like to go with me to take Chris on a Jet Ski ride. The kids were just finishing lunch and as we walked under the big oak tree to see them, Chris knocked over his plate. His aunt laughed and said, "When he sees you he jumps with excitement." We did not have to ask Chris twice whether he wanted to go on that Jet Ski ride. Chris absolutely loves the water and especially loves Jet Skis.

For someone with Chris's physical challenges, it is important to ride three to a Jet Ski so that he can be secure in the middle. The first order from Chris was to "go fast." Of course that directive was followed without any hesitation, and we soon received our first warning of the day for speeding away from the pier.

Continuing to follow our orders to go fast, we pretty much made a nuisance of ourselves to every water skier or boat that was unlucky enough to be in our path. Then, in a moment I will always treasure, Chris tapped my shoulder several times and as I leaned back to see what he wanted to say, he rested his head on my shoulder and very quietly said, "Let's just go slow."

Time stood still as the three of us silently drifted along the calm lake on that beautiful day. It is a moment that I wish could have lasted forever. I realize now, that moment will be forever.

At the end of another special day, we all said our good-byes and it was then that I recalled the words told to me by an old friend, "For those who love, there are no goodbyes, for we are forever connected in our hearts."

A few days after the event, I received a letter from the volunteer who rode with Chris:

> *Thank you so much for including me in the Dreams for Kids' family. It was such an exhilarating day for me. You have given kids with disabilities the opportunity to be "kids" and enjoy something as simple as going for a boat ride, or a Jet Ski ride, or even, God forbid an actual chance at skiing.*
>
> *These kids have a whole day when they can toss aside their ACL's and crutches and wheelchairs and just be a kid. A day when these kids are surrounded by other kids, just like them. For once, they are the "in" crowd, the majority. They are respected, honored and cherished for all of their Abilities. We, in fact, are forced to step out of our world and up into theirs. It's an enlightening and rewarding experience that's very hard to capture in mere words.*
>
> *As a parent of a special needs child, I can tell you how unique your organization is and how honored I am to have been a part of one special day.*
>
> *Thank you*
> *Shawna Egan*

Sailing Away from the Chair

> *How wonderful that no one need wait a single moment to improve the world.*
>
> ~ Anne Frank

As the summer winds begin to fade and the air turns brisk at night, there is more than just fall in the air—school is right around the corner. There is no better time than this to take a sail, way out on the expansive waters of Lake Michigan, along the fabulous Chicago Skyline.

Our annual day of sailing begins at Burnham Harbor, graciously sponsored by Judd Goldman Adaptive Sailing.

Surrounded by the largest of luxury boats and yachts, the kids throw a line in the water and try to catch that elusive fish. We are not counting on the catch to be our lunch, so a barbecue at water's edge is the order of the day.

Near the end of lunch, the kids suddenly become quiet and still as the adaptive sailboats, six in all, approach the pier.

The sailboats are large, but the type that allows you to touch the water if you lean over the side, an experience some of the kids will have that day. Each boat is also equipped with special chairs to strap in kids who do not have the ability to hold themselves upright.

This particular day was an especially beautiful one, with a slight breeze on calm waters, the sun periodically breaking through passing white clouds. As we loaded up the kids onto each of the sailboats, I got into the last boat and remember thinking how perfect the sky and landscape appeared.

As the parade of boats left the harbor, I could not help but smile at the sight. Six boats full of the most excited and happy kids you will ever find, sailing toward the free and open waters of Lake Michigan.

As the large boats from the harbor passed alongside of us, their captains waved, smiled, and said "Hi."

As the winds caught our sails, the kids cheered. As we sailed away, the sun broke through the clouds and was shining brilliantly. I turned back, and will always feel blessed that I did, for there was the most beautiful and breathtaking sight...*a pier full of empty wheelchairs.*

18

"Has Anyone Seen My Friend George...?"

We shall not cease from exploration, and the end of all our exploring will be to arrive where we started and know the place for the first time.

~ T. S. Elliot

I received a call in my office on December 16, 2005, from a young mother who said she lived in Cabrini-Green with her son. The woman explained that she had tried to get on the list for our upcoming 17th Annual Christmas Party for underprivileged and homeless children, but was told by Jesse White's office that the busses were full.

There is something about turning away a mother and her son at Christmas. It never happens on our watch. Having learned from the master himself, I told the woman, "Call Mr. White's office again, tell them that you spoke to me and I said to squeeze them in a little tighter on the bus."

I did not hear from the woman again, but I should have known that this story had only just begun.

Back to the Future

Never doubt that a small group of thoughtful, committed citizens can change the world. Indeed, it is the only thing that ever has.

~ Margaret Mead

On Christmas Eve, in the year 1989, a group of friends had huddled inside a tiny shelter in Englewood. We waited for fifty-four homeless children, who *had* been told that it was Christmas, to come downstairs and meet the guy in the red suit, who was standing outside in the cold with a bag full of gifts slung over his shoulder.

It was the year 2005, and Dreams for Kids was in final preparation to host 1,200 homeless and underprivileged children in the largest Christmas Party of its kind in Illinois.

How some things had changed in sixteen years, yet, in many ways, had still remained the same. Prosperity had been the buzzword for the greater part of those sixteen years, yet that word had hardly been the buzz for an even greater number of needy children than ever before.

So with each passing year, the Dreams for Kids' party site became larger. That year we landed in kid paradise, thanks to our host, Health World Children's Museum, an 85,000 square foot facility located in Barrington, Illinois. We took over the entire facility and its hundreds of interactive and educational children's exhibits.

When I arrived at the facility the night before our party, the General, Jim Smith, was fully engaged in event preparation mode. As the lobby set was being built by faculty and students from J.J.'s former high school, Loyola Academy, many other committed volunteers were hard at work. My brother Jim, his wife Maureen and their four children were assigned the task of alphabetizing 1,500 nametags. When I approached their table, my brother held up a single nametag out of the massive number of alphabetized and categorized names and told me that he had no idea which group it belonged to. The name on the tag was DeShawn, the son of the woman who called my office earlier that day.

I was just happy to know the woman who called my office was able to make the list, and before I could give it more thought, I was taken in by the flurry of activity as we prepared for the big day.

As Dick Marak unloaded 1,200 shopping bags full of gifts, craft tables were assembled on multiple floors, while four Santa stations were constructed in strategic locations. It had all the feeling of the North Pole and the spirit of St. Nick was in the air.

Winter Wonderland

In the early morning of December 17, 2005, all across Illinois, over 1,200 kids had either not slept a wink, or were just waking up. They were getting ready for the arrival of a bus to take them to a party that they would talk about for years.

The children would come from Englewood, from upstairs in Clara's House, Cabrini-Green, Chicago's Westside, Pilsen and Austin neighborhoods, and from numerous children's shelters. There would be children at the party from RIC, ICRE, and from the suburban Boys and Girls Clubs. They would come from all over the state, yet they also would share a common space, one desperate for the spirit of Christmas.

One hundred and fifty passionate volunteers had been up since dawn on this special day, working hard on the final event preparations.

When the first bus arrived, one hundred wide-eyed children stepped off that bus and into a fantasy. When the front doors of Health World opened, it was to the sounds of an entire high school choir singing Christmas carols, in the midst of an elaborate Winter Wonderland. As the children entered this magical scene, they passed through an Honor Guard suited for royalty.

Inspired by their fellow Marine's example, and their own unique sense of honor, an entourage of Marines from Corporal Marak's base, MTACS Great Lakes Naval Base, reported to Health World Children's Museum at daybreak. Reporting on their personal time, a Private First Class, two Corporals, a Staff Sergeant, a Lieutenant, a Captain, the Base Commanding Officer, and a "full bird" Colonel flanked the facility's entrance, and formed the most impressive Honor Guard you could ever hope to witness.

What a magnificent sight it was to see the expressions on the kid's faces, as they walked into paradise. These children were a bus ride away from abject poverty and homelessness, and were now being saluted, in honor, by the United States Marines.

For the next five hours, these children were our guests. In the spirit of what Dreams for Kids has always stood for, they were treated as if they were guests in our own homes. They were given a home for Christmas.

Toward the end of the day, as the last children dragged their bag of gifts to the door, J.J. had finally run out of candy to pass out to the departing guests and he called me over. As we talked about the day, J.J. told me that he had to share the most amazing story. J.J. said the story was about a six-year-old boy whom he had met. "His name was DeShawn…"

Nice to Meet You George

Coincidence is God's way of staying anonymous.
~ Goethe

As J.J. began to tell his story, I knew he had been significantly moved by this experience. Being convinced a long time ago that there are no real coincidences in this world; I was prepared to feel the same way.

Midway through the party, J.J. was on the lower level of the facility and a six-year-old boy walked up to him and said, "Hi, my name is DeShawn." J.J. introduced himself and DeShawn called him George. "I have no idea why he insisted that my name was George. I had replied to him, 'My name is J.J.,' and then he said 'Nice to meet you George.' That was it. I was George. I figured he was six years old, I could be George."

As J.J. and DeShawn were talking, DeShawn put his hands on the arm of J.J.'s chair and asked, 'Are you *really* in a wheelchair?' "I did not know what he meant by that, until I looked around and noticed empty wheelchairs and realized that we were in the disability exhibit section. DeShawn must have thought I was an instructor. I told him, 'Yes, I am really in a wheelchair.'"

DeShawn told J.J. that he was "very sorry that he was in a wheelchair." When J.J. told him not to be sorry, because he was happy and he was alright, DeShawn's face brightened and he suddenly asked, "Will you play with me George?"

So off they went, DeShawn and George, brand new friends, as they explored the facility and its many exhibits. When they arrived at the rainforest, DeShawn sailed down the huge slide and then slowly walked up to J.J., put his hand back on J.J.'s chair, leaned in close and said, "It makes me sad that you are in a wheelchair, George."

J.J. told DeShawn, "I don't want you to be sad. I am okay and I am having fun playing with you." DeShawn then asked, "Will you wait in line with me to see Santa Claus, George?" As they walked together to see Santa, DeShawn put his hand on J.J.'s back and said, "I want to give you my gift from Santa, George." In one of the rare moments in his life, J.J. was at a loss for words. After a pause, he said, "I can't accept your present from Santa, DeShawn. Santa picked it out just for you." When DeShawn said he really wanted to give him his present, J.J. asked DeShawn if he had made a craft and said, "You could give me your craft."

Hearing J.J. say this, DeShawn smiled and ran to the craft

table. DeShawn came back with a red star, sprinkled with silver glitter—and a large pin. "Whether someone is six or sixty, they hardly ever think the paralyzed guy can feel anything, so I knew I was in trouble," J.J. said. After three or four painful attempts, he asked DeShawn if maybe a grown-up might be able help. "Sure enough, one of the volunteers took over right where DeShawn had left off, but, thankfully, we finally found my shirt and I was never happier to see a little red star on my chest."

As J.J. told me this magnificent story, I told him that I had another chapter to share. I told him about the phone call I had received, and about the nametag, and, as J.J.'s eyes widened, I then told him about Devon.

Devon Coleman is one of Father Wally's original kids, now all grown up and prosperous. Devon had come up to me just a short time earlier, as the party was winding down, and said that he had to tell me about the "greatest thing" he had seen. Devon had seen J.J. and DeShawn together, and had watched them from afar. "I saw them during the party, and it was really something to watch. This little kid had his hand on the arm of J.J.'s wheelchair and they were just hanging out everywhere. These two guys could not have been more different. A little black kid, from one of the really hard neighborhoods or shelters, and an older white guy in a wheelchair, and they were just hanging out like they had known each other forever."

Devon continued, "It looked so cool that I left to find a camera, but when I returned, they were gone and I could never find them again. A little while later, I see the little guy and he is all upset. He is saying, over and over again, 'Has anyone seen my friend George?' He was really upset, and was wringing his hands and everything. He kept saying that he could not find George anywhere and he just had to find him." Devon said he felt bad he could not help DeShawn. "I had no idea who George was."

As I told J.J. this story, he smiled. "I was here at the front door, saying goodbye to all the kids and passing out the candy. All of a sudden, there was DeShawn and his mom. DeShawn yelled, 'George!' and ran to me and he gave me a huge hug. DeShawn then looked down at my shirt and got all excited. 'You still have my craft George!'" J.J. continued with a look on his face that I had seen from him several times over the years, a look of recognition and gratitude that he had been visited by a moment of grace.

"The star was pinned right over my heart, and DeShawn put both his hands over it, looked me in the eye, and said, 'I want you to always keep my craft right here George. When you look at it, you will remember me.' DeShawn's mom called him from the door and he ran to her, but just before he left the building, he turned and smiled, and said, 'Merry Christmas, George!'"

We All Are Who We Once Were...

The important thing is this: To be able at any moment to sacrifice what we are for what we could become.
~ Charles Dubois

After each of our Christmas parties, I usually spend time reflecting on the day's events and their significance. In 2005, I was to realize the great distance from which we had come, and also how the road which we traveled had now come full circle. We had begun on a mother's request and had then applied the training of mentors who now seem mythical.

As the reach of our organization had broadened, the path had been lit by a brilliant introduction into the hidden world of those with disabilities. In retrospect, the transition appeared seamless, yet it was an education every step of the way.

It has been said we all are who we once were. Dreams for Kids is indeed what it has always been: A magnificent collection of thoughtful, committed citizens, doing their part to change the world. Dreams for Kids is so much more than what we were. It was the magical visit of a six-year-old boy that reminded us of what we have become.

In a suburb of Chicago, a few days before Christmas, in the year 2005, an expansive children's fantasyland was filled with every single representative of a sixteen-year journey. There was *Clara Kirk*, still sheltering after all these years, *Father Wally's* kids were there, all grown up and giving back. There was *J.J.*, *Dick Marak*, and *Jim Smith* and, of course, there were the kids: wheeling and walking in, from north, south, east and west, all colors, ages, gender and abilities, joined as one group, with no differences to separate them.

Walking the streets of the "soul coast" from dawn to dusk was *Jesse White*, delivering 10,000 Christmas dinners. Presiding over the entire day was the ever-present spirit of the giant influence of a small priest and a special mom, *Father Wally* and *Patricia Tuohy*.

A six-year-old boy appeared with a message and "made George a star," to remind us of how far we had traveled. It was this boy's gift that also reminded us of how much more we could become.

We never found DeShawn again, and part of me knew we never would. As much as we tried to locate him, DeShawn was not on the original guest roster and there is no record of him or his mom ever having lived in Cabrini-Green.

DeShawn showed up in the way that he did for reasons that are all too clear. Long ago, I stopped denying the presence of the special grace that moments of destiny bring to our lives. For everything there is a time, and for all visitors to our lives there is a reason. DeShawn's visit was an image that will last a lifetime.

George represents an entire society of those who live in the isolation of poverty or other disabilities, but whose isolation can be broken by opportunity and the dolphin spirit of compassion and acceptance.

DeShawn represents the very best in all of us; someone who has little of his own, yet gives what he has to someone who has less.

I have never been more convinced that we can change the world for the better. In another seventeen years, if we are still looking for the answer, at least now we know the right question: *Has anyone seen my friend George?*

They say dolphins rarely use their eyes to see. The dolphin leads with its heart and senses those in need and embraces them with compassion and acceptance.

For one brief, brilliant, moment in time, DeShawn found George and they became friends and all differences in age, race, ability, poverty, and social status ceased to exist. There was nothing at all to see past, for all that could be seen was a shining star, and the brilliant light of compassion and acceptance that gives hope for the true dolphin spirit that lives in us all.

Merry Christmas, George, wherever you are...

19

Dream Leaders

The future has a way of arriving unannounced.
~ George Will

In early 2006 I attended a conference in Orlando. After leaving early to catch a flight, I noticed two familiar faces in the airport security line. As we removed our shoes, a young lady smiled and said she recognized me from the conference. After introducing myself as being with Dreams for Kids, she said with a big smile, "We're from Free The Children."

Free The Children is based in Toronto and acclaimed as the world's largest organization of young people helping young people. When Amy Schlein continued, "Our organization was founded eleven years ago by Craig Kielburger when he was twelve years old," I could only hope, for the first time ever that the security line would slow down. It turns out, not only were they walking towards Gate 48, they were connecting in Chicago. We were flying on the same plane.

It proved to be another extraordinary meeting of destiny. My wish for a flight delay was granted and, for the next ninety minutes, I listened to the extraordinary story of how a twelve-year-old boy took a stand against child labor and poverty. Addressing his seventh grade class, he declared, "This can't happen in the world we live in and us do nothing. Who will join me?" So began an historic mission that would result in Free The Children building over 500 schools in sixteen developing countries around the world, and Craig being nominated four times for the Nobel Peace Prize.

When it was my turn to share the story of Dreams for Kids, Russ McLeod listened intently and said, "There is a need for what you do in every country we have been. Those with disabilities in the developing world are invisible. They do not exist in society." Russ, who is the executive director of Me to We Books/Music, a social enterprise created by Craig and his brother Marc to support the work of Free The Children, continued, "We will help with your global expansion." Next would be the question that set the stage for the rest of my life. Completely without judgment, Russ asked, "Why aren't you doing this full time?"

This was an opportunity for me to choose between an established law career and what could make the greatest difference in the world. Russ and Amy were sitting near the front of the plane. When we arrived in Chicago, true to their characters, they were waiting at the gate to give me, in their words, "a proper goodbye." They both gave me a hug. I told Russ my choice was made in one short plane ride—to leave my law practice and direct the global expansion of Dreams for Kids

Russ invited me to the Free The Children offices in Toronto and to meet their staff. Over the course of several visits, Russ generously introduced me to their programs and methodology, and to the way of life this extraordinary organization has created across the world.

Back in Chicago, we considered what we had learned and imagined the possibilities. As an organization, we were at an inflection point. Reflecting on our history, we knew we never could have charted the course we travelled. It would have been impossible to have envisioned on Christmas Eve, 1989, what we eventually would become. Looking back now, it is clear that those who came before us were born to lead us to this point. Just as the mentors of my life were indispensable to whom I had become, Dreams for Kids was the sum of all the parts of an extraordinary collection of humanitarians. Now, it was the wisdom of youth that revealed the path we should travel.

Once again, we were called upon to deepen our mission and to expand our reach. Realizing we were serving the most isolated kids on earth—those living in poverty and those with disabilities—it was time to unite them with their peers. Although our plan was to bring the most diverse kids together to serve in a youth leadership program, we had learned our lesson long ago. If this was to be their program, we needed to listen. In two unforgettable visits, we discovered the wisdom of a generation desperate to be heard. Soon, the world would be listening.

"Who Can We Help?"

If I am not for myself, who will be for me? But if I am only for myself, who am I? If not now, when?

~ Hillel

It was easy for us to envision the impact of a youth leadership program that unites a diverse generation. If given the opportunity to serve and grow together, beyond the walls and divisions of segregation and infused with the spirit of service, compassion, and understanding, it would stand to reason that it would be impossible to judge others. If given opportunity, we all would see past wheelchairs, skin color, and religious belief. Imagine if a generation grew up with that vision. The world would transform; conflict would be unimaginable, and peace would be inevitable. This was the grand vision of our program. Soon we would discover its heart and soul. Of course, first we had to listen to the kids. We knew where we would begin. It would be where it all began for us twenty years ago.

We went to the Southside of Chicago, to Harlan Community Academy, a school with one of the highest poverty rates in the city. While it is impossible to get an accurate count of a statistic that increases significantly each year, there are currently a record 12,525 homeless students in the Chicago Public schools alone, according to the Chicago Coalition for the Homeless. According to The National Center on Family Homelessness, there are an estimated 1.5 million homeless children in the United States, one out of every fifty kids. At Harlan, that figure has been estimated to be as high as twenty percent of all students.

When we arrived at Harlan's AVID (Advancement Via Individual Determination) program, we shared our vision with the students and invited them to be our first leaders. Their collective response was engaged and it was certain—"Who can we help?" Their passion took us a little by surprise. They were waiting to be asked.

We shared some stories about the students we were working with at ICRE, the Illinois Center for Recreation and Rehabilitation, where Carmen Villafane lived. They were fascinated and wanted to know more. Diversity is not the word to describe Harlan's student body. Almost 100 percent of the students are African American. Most live in poverty. There were no kids with disabilities in the entire school. The students asked why there were no kids like the kids in ICRE in their school. They wanted to know more about their lives.

As we shared about ICRE, we told the Harlan students that the ICRE kids were fundraising so they could go deep-sea diving in Key Largo, Florida. Diveheart, our longtime partner, provides children, adults, and wounded veterans the opportunity to leave their wheelchairs and experience the pure freedom of the water. To Diveheart's founder Jim Elliot, it is a mission: "We teach people to fly." The year before, Jim and his group brought a group of ICRE students to this bit of paradise and the trip became a dream for every kid at ICRE.

We explained to the Harlan students that the ICRE kids were having a difficult time because it is hard to fundraise for yourself. Harlan kids huddled up. When they returned, they handed us their lunch money. One of the students told us they knew it would not be enough, so they wanted to fundraise. After school, they took to the streets of one of the poorest neighborhoods in the city and proved it was not poor in spirit. They raised $1,000.

To show the Harlan kids that generosity is rewarded, we leveraged this amount by requesting a match from the Jeff Lawless Foundation. We brought $2,000 to ICRE and told the students, "This is what your peers did for you." Immediately the ICRE kids asked the same question, "Who can we help?" This time we were prepared. We showed them a film of kids in Kenya who, like most kids in developing countries, had no wheelchairs. They were crawling in the dust. The ICRE kids cried. Sitting in all they owned, they could not believe any kid in the world would not have a wheelchair.

That weekend, the ICRE kids baked cookies, set up tables on Roosevelt Road, and held a bake sale. They raised $540 and sent two wheelchairs to Africa.

Right before our eyes, the program came alive. Just as we had a feeling the first day at Clara's House, and later felt a similar feeling with the first activity of Extreme Recess, we knew this was a moment. It was the beginning of something extraordinary. The Harlan and ICRE kids had given our idea a beating heart and instilled into our program a deep purpose. It was clear who they were and where they could lead us. This could be the start of a movement the world had never seen before. These were our Dream Leaders.

One Kid at a Time

> *No one is born a good citizen; no nation is born a democracy. Rather, both are processes that continue to evolve over a lifetime. Young people must be included from birth. A society that cuts off from its youth severs its lifeline.*
>
> ~ Kofi Annan

It was a revelation, a true paradigm shift. What can seem so obvious to all of us now had escaped the experts for years. The most isolated and, in many cases, completely forgotten kids only need opportunity. It is the opportunity to give. It is in giving that we all find our true power, our most intrinsic value. Given the opportunity to help others, kids' lives are literally transformed. They are no longer victims. They are not the problem. They are the solution.

We were soon to find out how many kids were waiting to be found, how many voices were waiting to be heard. The surprises continued for us, as students from some of the most privileged areas in the country expressed a similar desire to be heard and voiced similar frustrations of being misunderstood and being labeled. A common desire among them was the belief that they could make a difference in the world. They wanted to be given the opportunity.

Knowing that true diversity cannot be found in most neighborhoods or in most schools, we created the Dreams Leaders Conference to bring together the most diverse kids. For an entire day, youth from every race, religious background, social class, and disability show up to be reminded how powerful they are and how much the world needs them. It is a magical day. The day is filled with workshops and leadership training. It is a day that introduces them to social and cultural awareness, local and global issues, and the type of peer interaction they waited a lifetime to experience. At the end of a life-changing eight-hour day, an auditorium full of emotional youth hold their candles high and commit to never again failing to see the possibility of their life or place in the world. It is followed by an entire year of service, working alongside a group of ten of their most diverse peers, and taking on projects that impact their local and global communities.

Every Dreams Leaders Conference, every day, there are more extraordinary young people taking a stand.

Cortez was born on Christmas Day. He weighed 1 pound 7 ounces. His mother was a drug addict. His father was in prison. After months in the hospital, he was released to the care of his grandmother. He grew up confused and angry. He literally fought his way through school. He suffered from abuse. However, he said he did not find out how badly he could be beaten until his father got out of prison. One day Cortez found out about the Dream Leaders program while he was surfing the Internet. He asked if he could join.

In the six months following his conference, Cortez began a breathtaking series of projects. He wrote a position paper on the Middle East because he had met Muslim youth, realized they were much different than what he had heard, and wanted his peers to know the truth. He hosted exchange students from Serbia. He made plans to host an Arab-American youth conference at the Chicago Cultural Center. He started a blog called Breaking Perceptions. He was elected vice president of his senior class.

Two months later, Cortez Alexander was accepted into Seton Hall University. Today he simply says, "I am going to change the world."

George suffered through a half-dozen abusive foster parents. In one home he was beaten, burned, and left on a basement floor in a locked and dark room for weeks. After attending his conference, George became one of our youth speakers. He wanted to inspire his peers. He became a captain for our community service initiatives and he organized fundraisers to help children living in poverty. He returned to the Dreams Leaders Conferences to volunteer as a facilitator. He stood before his peers from across the state to say, "Being a Dream Leader means being a person who goes out of their way to help someone in need, to look at the world with open hands and open eyes, to inspire millions of people who are pushed aside because of their race, social class, or disabilities. This is what it means to me. We are going to make a difference in the world."

Over the years, Dream Leaders Conferences have unveiled a surprising truth—that young people from every demographic face very similar issues. It is a reminder of how related we all are. One might think the hot button of being labeled was limited to those living in poverty or with a disability. It turns out that kids, even from the most privileged social class, struggle and resent being labeled. They too feel isolated and misunderstood.

What is most inspiring is that each of them has a common desire, a burning passion to change the world. They want to know more about each other. They see beyond the walls of segregation and now see each other for who they truly are. It is a generation that wants to work together to celebrate their differences. They see the world as how it can be. They share a common dream. It is a dream whose time has come.

A Dream Realized

The whole course of human history may depend on a change of heart in one solitary and even humble individual—for it is in the solitary mind and soul of the individual that the battle between good and evil is waged and ultimately won or lost.

~ M. Scott Peck

On May 18, 2009, I was checking my mail on LinkedIn and there was a note that read, "I have worked for 25-plus years in international development and have always had a central focus on youth in global impact. I am interested in the work you are doing through Dreams for Kids." Kevin McFarland

How could it be known this was another moment of transformation? Having lived in the space of extraordinary life-changing possibility for so long, I certainly was open to anything. However the meetings and events that alter the very course of our lives are most clearly seen while looking back. In the present we can only have hope for the future.

In one phone call, we both knew. On my end, it was an introduction to one of the world's great humanitarians and brilliant strategic planners. For Kevin, he admitted to seeing, "A twenty-eight-year-old dream sitting on a dusty shelf, and whose time had come."

In 1983, Kevin McFarland was studying for his Ph.D. at Stanford University. One day he had a conversation with a fifteen-year-old girl that changed his life in a single moment. It was also a conversation that changed the world.

The girl was working with Kevin in a school youth program. She was passionately sharing that much more had to be done for the poor of the world and they needed to start an organization to do it. Kevin began to explain why that simply was not practical: "In order to effectively integrate into another culture and impact lives, we need to know much more than we do now about economics, engineering, agriculture, politics, and finance."

The girl stopped him, looked up, and said, "You don't have to know all that stuff. You just have to know that people are dying in a world that has more than enough. And it is breaking God's heart. We have to do whatever it takes. Even if it kills us, we have to do something."

Kevin was stunned. He recalls going from a sense of satisfaction that his answer was so adult-like in ruling out such idealism, to suddenly becoming present to a sense of purpose and urgency more clear than anything he had ever experienced.

The next day, amid protests from those close to him and

a chorus of disbelief and doubt, Kevin ended his studies and dropped out of Stanford. He followed the wisdom of this young girl and founded a youth organization, Manna International. As is common in times of transition, Kevin was uncertain of where this path might lead. However he knew it was where his heart was leading him.

Over the next twenty-two years, his organization worked in thirty-two developing countries and become one of the coordinating NGOs on the ground for the last twenty-three global disaster relief operations, from Ethiopia to New Orleans. His youth organization provided emergency relief, drilled thousands of wells, reconstructed vast regions, rescued entire villages, and saved millions of lives.

Kevin told me, "I learned early in our global work that, in giving a starving person a bag of rice, we were saving lives. However, I also knew we were taking away their livelihood. Consequently, we worked with sustainable solutions that empowered people to be self-sufficient." However, the sheer enormity of suffering and scale of challenges in the developing world convinced Kevin to begin work as a consultant for multinational institutions working on creating partnerships for multibillion dollar sustainable economic development projects.

Still, Kevin's heart was with his twenty-eight-year-old dream, sitting on a dusty shelf.

Over the course of several conversations, Kevin's growing understanding of Dreams for Kids, and where we were headed, reminded him of the work he did in the field. It reignited his long-standing belief in the capacity of youth. In the stories of our Dream Leaders, he knew this was the generation he had dreamed of. He knew this was the generation that could completely change the world.

It was during his work in the most desperate places in the world that Kevin witnessed the astounding capacity of youth who lived amid horrific atrocities. He saw in them what the kids at Harlan and ICRE showed us.

Kevin told me that youth in the developing world, while living with unimaginable suffering, were as generous as anyone he had ever encountered. He recalled, "In 1986, I was doing relief work in El Salvador. We were providing assistance to some of the nearly one million people who had been internally displaced as a result of the civil war. I was in a camp that stretched for miles in the capital city. On either side of the railroad tracks people were living in shacks made of cardboard, sticks and mud."

One day, as Kevin was saying his goodbyes, an eleven-year-old boy asked why he had to leave. Kevin explained, "I have to go to Ethiopia because children are dying due to the famine." The boy said, "Please wait right here." He went behind a blanket that served as a wall between the shacks. When he returned he had in his hands a page from a magazine. When people lose everything and must live in mere cardboard shacks, they often tear out pages from magazines so they can decorate their walls to help make it feel like home.

The little boy reached up and handed Kevin the page. It was a photo of an emaciated Ethiopian child. He looked into Kevin's eyes and said, "Bring him to us. We will feed him."

As I reflected on this amazing story, Kevin said, "I have witnessed countless acts of selfless generosity by young people living in the poorest places on earth. In your Dream Leaders I see their dreams. I know now; this is the time to unite them. This generation can be the solution. There is destiny in them."

Over the next year, Kevin became a central part of the Dreams for Kids family. Together, we created strategic plans for the global expansion of Dreams for Kids and moved one step closer to the realization of a long-lost dream of an extraordinary humanitarian.

Empowering a Generation

Few will have the greatness to bend history itself; but each of us can work to change a small portion of events, and in the total of all those acts will be written the history of this generation.

~ Robert F. Kennedy

We live in one of the most challenging times in human history. The mere thought of attempting to solve the critical sector issues that threaten our quality of life, and even our very survival, can seem daunting. That is one way to look at it. I prefer to see this time as the most exciting and promising in all of history. We are called to the greatest challenge and, if we respond in ways we are capable, we will create a sustainable world of shared prosperity. We can end absolute poverty. We can stop the exploitation of children. We can advance human rights in such a way that it will be unthinkable there was ever an issue.

One thing is very certain. We will do none of this if each of us does not do our part. Perhaps it has been born of necessity; however, never before has collaboration among for-profit and nonprofit leaders been embraced in the way it is today. Social entrepreneurship is no longer just a concept; it is now a viable way to prosper and change the world. Leading academic institutions, such as Northwestern University and Stanford, have opened their doors and resources to create institutes that share best practices. The Kellogg Innovation Network (KIN) created the KIN Global Summit to encourage dialogue and action through innovative solutions to humanity's greatest challenges.

Individuals are seeking a place to make a difference. There is a longing for true fulfillment, and more people are realizing it is found in giving and in service. The truth is: we need everyone. Imagine the possibilities if each of us followed the creed of Jesse White and did at least one good thing for one person every single day. Imagine if we harnessed that energy and good will and created a strategy for solution rather than complaint, for engagement rather than indifference. The world would transform.

As we gather momentum, we must remember the generation to which we are dedicated. They have no desire to wait. There are hundreds of millions of young people who might seem to be the most unlikely source for solution, unless we see them differently. Unless we see them for who they are. We can empower them by giving each of them the opportunity to "be the difference" today. We can unite them as an unstoppable force of change and good will. We can give them their power by hearing their voices. If we no longer see them as the problem and, instead, engage them as the solution, they will be empowered beyond measure. They can change the world if we only let them.

The Harlan/ICRE story and the Dream Leader movement have ignited an engagement of action that inspires us every day. IBM has come forward to create a global partnership and project-building website to bring this generation together online, so that they may share culture and build community change projects across all barriers of distance and social class. Everywhere Kevin goes, from the United Nations and the World Bank to the leading academic and multinational organizations, the response is the same: "How can we work together?"

Each day brings a call from more individuals and organizations. From India to South Africa and from the UK to Canada, the question is the same: "How can we engage our youth?" The Dreams for Kids event, which began on Christmas Eve, 1989, in Clara's House, is now called Holiday for Hope and is hosted by people of all faith in more than thirty cities and villages around the world.

In every community, in every corner of the earth, there are young people whose voices are waiting to be heard. It will indeed be the sum total of the acts of each one of us that will determine our future. If we unite in support of them and truly empower this generation of youth, they may very well bend history.

What will your role be? How will you engage and be the change you wish to see in the world?

Bringing Out the Best in Ourselves

When we seek to discover the best in others, we somehow bring out the best in ourselves.

~ William Arthur Ward

On October 16, 2009, Dreams for Kids celebrated our twentieth anniversary. The event was held at Chicago's historic Planetarium. Under the stars above were the real stars within.

As is our custom, the kids were a big part of it all. It began immediately. Walking and rolling side by side, behind the pageantry of the bagpipers, they marched in, carrying flags, to a standing ovation. Several kids remarked later that it was the proudest moment of their lives. No one had ever asked any of them to carry a flag. Representing the diversity of life, they represent those flags better than anyone can. This is not how the world could look; this is how the world does look.

Of course, Cortez and George were there. Crystal, with the widest smile you will ever see, rolled in, wearing her magnificent white dress and holding the Dreams for Kids flag. Then there was Tyler.

The program was arranged to show a twenty-year journey in narrative, with photos and video. At select times the spotlight shifted from the stage to the audience, and history came to life. One such time came during our Extreme Recess video. While showing a photo montage of kids experiencing sports they had long since been denied, the video abruptly stopped in the middle of the song. The image was of a thirteen-year-old boy sitting in an adaptive water ski at pier's edge and getting ready for the time of his life. He was wearing green goggles. He had a grin from ear to ear.

As the video and music froze, the spotlight lit up Tyler Woodworth in the audience. He was standing. He was wearing his green goggles. Like a seasoned pro, Tyler waited for the laughter and applause to fall silent, and then he started to speak.

Tyler has some form of disability. We all have some form of disability, something we are unable to do. Every one of us also has ability, and that is what counts. Tyler's disability has given him an uncertain balance and a voice uniquely his own. It has also given him a charisma and spirit that are captivating. Before the evening began, I met with Tyler and his dad, and we attempted to coach Tyler for his big moment. He nodded his head and, later, we were happy to find out, he ignored everything we said.

Tyler simply said, "Because of Dreams for Kids I could actually sit behind a boat and say to the driver, 'Gun it.' I did. And he did. Now doors are open for me. And when they don't open, I just open them myself."

A friend of mine pulled me aside later in the evening and said, "That young boy gave me one of the greatest gifts of my life. When he started to speak, I grabbed the edge of the table and thought, 'Please God, let this boy be understood.' Then I immediately became present to the fact that this was exactly what I thought every time my father spoke since his illness. I realized for the first time that I had been judging my father. He was the same person he had always been, just trying to communicate as best he could. This was my father who raised me and who loved me. And I judged him. The tears rolled down my face. I bowed my head and asked my father to forgive me and I made a promise to never again judge another human being."

My friend said that, when he raised his head, something remarkable happened, "I listened. And I understood every single word that boy said."

Thank you, Tyler, for being the messenger that reminds us all to listen without judgment. Thank you for inspiring us to see the best in you, and bring out the best in ourselves.

A Generation of Destiny

Every great dream begins with a dreamer. Always remember, you have within you the strength, the patience, and the passion to reach for the stars to change the world.

~ Harriet Tubman

Twenty years later, it feels as if we have just begun. The future stretches out before us and what we see fills us with hope. We have learned from those who came before us, and we have gained immeasurable wisdom from those who have come after us.

We will be led by a generation of youth born to change the world. They live in your community. They live in distant villages. They may even live in your own home. If we listen without judgment, we can hear them. If our vision is clear, we can see them from the inside. We can unite them as no generation has ever been. We can empower them in ways the world has never seen. They can create the world of our dreams.

If you doubt whether this is possible, or if you should even dare to hope, consider your place in history. There will never be a time such as this. With unity of purpose and individual engagement, the future is ours to create. You can change a life. That life can change a generation of lives.

If there ever comes a time when you question whether your contribution can make a difference or whether you even have something to give, I hope you will remember Shamique. Shamique lives in ICRE. She has cerebral palsy and uses a wheelchair. One day Abby, our Dream Leaders director, asked the students at ICRE to assemble for an exercise. Many of the kids have difficulty using their hands so she asked the kids to take some clay and to form letters. Each of them followed the instructions and formed the letters CANNOT. When they finished, she asked them to discuss how many people had told them they cannot do something. It was a spirited discussion.

Then Abby said she wanted them all to raise their hands and, on her cue, lower them and smash the "nots" out of their lives. On cue, the room exploded in youthful energy. When they were done smashing the negativity from their lives, some of the kids were angry. Many of them were crying. And all of them were free.

Shamique rolled forward and said, "Ms. Abby, I know what my dream is now. I want to be able to have a job." When Abby asked what kind of job she wanted, Shamique looked up and said, "My eyes are good. I want to help blind people."

What gifts have you been given? What blessings do you have to share with others so they may be free?

Every person among us, from the young to the young at heart, is capable of making a difference. We all have ability. We all have something to give. It will be the sum total of our collective contribution that makes all the difference and creates a new world. There is a generation of youth waiting to lead us. They are reaching for the stars. They are showing us the way. Can you hear them?

It is time for us to take our stand.

Let's change the world.

Epilogue

*I may not have gone where I intended to go, but I think
I have ended up where I intended to be.*
~ Douglas Adams

I t can never be said that I charted this course. To say that I
could have imagined how this story would unfold and know
of the many gifts that would be given to me along the way, would
have been impossible. I had only hoped to help others, as I myself
had been helped. In the process, I have done my best to grow and
learn and become the person I was meant to be. As I continue
along that road, I wish to share with you one final story.

The question I have been asked most frequently is this: Why
did you start Dreams for Kids? I hope in telling this story that I
have answered that question. Always appreciating that the best
in theatre will give you opportunities to laugh, to cry, and to go
home thinking, I have tried to tell this story in a way which made
the characters come alive. Recognizing there is no substitute for
the truth and fact is always more amazing than fiction, I have, to
the very best of my recollections, not changed a word of fact.

George Bernard Shaw said, "Youth is wasted on the
young." Well, I can definitely say that a truly great gift which I
received in writing this book was to relive this story and the lessons of the influential teachers of my life, at a time when I have
a deeper appreciation and understanding of their impact on me
and others.

As I look back at the giants who towered over my early
life, I am humbled to see Father Wally, Jesse White, and Patricia
Tuohy. It is quite easy for me to conclude now, that starting and
sustaining Dreams for Kids was the *least* I could do to repay their
influence.

Being met along the way to this time and place by the magnificent influence of Clara Kirk, J.J. O'Connor, Jim Smith, Dick Marak, Carmen Villafane, Bob Lujano, over 30,000 hopeful and inspiring kids, and all those special people who graced their lives, could only have fueled my desire to continue along this road. Having received so much in return has been more reward than I ever deserved.

Writing the story of Dreams for Kids has helped define my life in ways that I had never imagined. Telling this story has also reinforced the lessons I have learned from so many great and gracious teachers. With those lessons, I have grown and become the person I am today. However, in traveling down the same path, I realized I still had some significant unfinished business.

Of all the gifts I have received on the way to this place, it seems there was one more gift that was left unopened, and it was in telling this story that I discovered it.

This is the final story and its gift. When I opened this unexpected gift, inside were the long lost dreams of an eight year old boy and a message of forgiveness.

> *Forgiveness is unlocking the door to set someone free and realizing you were the prisoner.*
>
> ~ Max Lucado

When I was a small boy, my father left and never came back. When my father walked away, he never wrote and he never called. When my father left our family and me, he gave my mother the title of "single parent." The future for my young mother and her four young children proved to be extremely difficult.

For many years, my mother struggled and worked two jobs. She did everything possible to hold our family together and to give us, her children, an opportunity for a future. We were forced to sell our home and experienced some desperate times, as my mother shouldered on with a determined dignity. I witnessed my mother rise in the morning, every single day, and face her challenges with unwavering commitment, towering strength, uncompromised character and, always, compassion for those who had less.

God blessed me with the good fortune and the opportunity to return the home to my mother that she lost. For a time, all too brief, I also helped return the comforts of life to her, for which she had lived without for so long.

As you can imagine, my feelings toward my father, and I had many, were not good. Initial confusion had given way to sadness, then to hurt, and then anger. Finally, as I processed this hardship as being part of my life, and appreciated the role it had in shaping who I had become, I arrived at acceptance. What was missing from my healing was the hardest to come by: *forgiveness*. That it was never a secret where my father was located, as he moved around the country, only compounded the problem.

I had spent the better part of my life firmly committed to never forgiving my father and I swore off all contact with him. This was not difficult since my father had never reached out to me. However, all the experts can hardly be wrong; failing to forgive someone is a tremendous burden to live with and it holds no value. The very nature of the Dreams for Kids' experience has been one of acceptance and compassion. As I wrote of the magnificent examples of these virtues, I was never more aware of what was missing in my own life and what I needed to do.

In June of that year, 2005, I journaled a commitment: To do what I considered to be the hardest thing in my life. I was going to seek out my father and do what was right.

In the early morning of Sunday, July 24th 2005, some forty years after my father had abandoned us and never returned, I sat in a booth in a restaurant and waited for my Dad.

As I looked out the restaurant window, it easily could have been 1965. If it were a film, I would have been that same eight-year-old boy in a flashback, looking out the front window of my house, waiting....

I had arrived twenty minutes early on that day, and the time spent waiting for my father's arrival moved at a surreal pace, as the years of my life unfolded in my mind. There was a point when I literally felt like I was that eight-year-old boy again. As time stood still, I would even feel that the other people in the restaurant saw me as this little boy, waiting alone in that booth.

While I was lost in deep thought, the waitress brought me back to the present when she asked if I was going to continue to wait for my party. I smiled and told her, "It's been awhile, but I think I can hold out for another five minutes."

In the final days before the scheduled meeting with my father, I had told few people. I had, however, taken the advice of a trusted friend, who had told me to leave any agenda I might have at home, and to walk in with an open mind. I took that advice to heart and simply tried to be open to whatever occurred. There would be no way for me to know how it would play out, and I had no clue what my immediate response would be when I saw my father again.

As my father walked in the front door, strangely enough, I recognized him immediately. As he looked around the restaurant, I waved to him. My father looked in my direction, and as he walked toward me I saw a seventy-nine-year-old man who was very nervous. Seeing this, I immediately sensed that there had been much pain in his life as well. Instinctively, I then did that which I had *never* considered possible. I got up and hugged my father.

We talked for over three hours, a father and his adult son, long strangers to each other's lives. It was a very powerful experience. I will be forever grateful for the advice that I received in preparing for that meeting. If I had not left myself open, I would never have been able to listen, to understand or learn. In listening to my father's story, I clearly understood, for the first time in my life, that my father was not capable of giving me what I had needed. It was not in him.

I was able to understand that no one would consciously choose to travel the road my father had traveled, with all of its consequences. Anyone on this road must have lived with his own pain and suffered greatly. I had to see past my own disabilities of anger, hurt, and abandonment. A young friend once told me, "There is too much hurt in the world. There is no point in letting what happened yesterday affect how you feel toward a person today, if they want to be a part of your life again."

I had the deep and grateful awareness that I had been prepared for this moment by a lifetime of experiences and by the dolphins of my life. I also felt a great sense of gratitude, knowing that everything which had transpired in my life had become reality because of my father's decision so many years ago.

There is no question it was my mother's dedication, guidance, and love that has defined the life I have lived. However, there can be little doubt that my father's absence played a significant role in the person I have become. It was my mother's suggestion I start Dreams for Kids. Yet the passion to sustain it surely was fueled in part by what was missing from my life.

With compassion, gratitude, and acceptance in my heart, there could be only one thing to do. I forgave my father. The hurt and pain of forty years just melted away.

I have spent the better part of my life consciously and creatively hiding from this story. Unlocking the door to forgiveness has now set free the desire to do just the opposite. If sharing this experience opens doors for others, its true value will far exceed the tremendous benefits it has given to me.

I thank you for traveling back in time with me. May your life be visited often by those special dolphin moments of grace.

Wherever you are George, may you never lose hope. There are dolphins in your life too. They may not have found you yet, but they will. When they do find you, they will make you a star. They will leave their craft on your heart so you will always remember there is compassion and acceptance in this world. Someday soon, just you wait and see, your dreams will come true too.

P.S. I love you Mom.

How You Can Change the World

The world changes one person at a time. Real, lasting change results from the actions of ordinary people making a difference, one day at a time. Change will not happen without taking action. You can make a world of difference today!

- Gather your family and friends and visit a local children's facility, homeless shelter, or nursing home. Ask in advance if they need clothing or supplies.

- Just say, "Hi!" Acknowledgement can be all too rare. Take a moment to call those you love and share your feelings. The next person you see using a wheelchair—smile and say, "Hi!"

- Encourage the young people in your life—they want to be engaged. Research local youth leadership programs or call Dreams for Kids and ask when our Dream Leaders Program will be in your area.

- Join the text revolution! You can help a charity with a donation as small as $10 by using your cell phone. To support Dreams for Kids, Text DREAMS to 80888. It is that simple. A charge of $10 will be added to your monthly cell phone bill.

- Remember those who are isolated around the holidays. Check the Dreams for Kids website to see if a Holiday for Hope celebration is being planned for your area. If there is not one listed, be the first to plan it!

- Collect canned goods, or other non-perishable items for a local food pantry.

- Host an environmental awareness day: recycle old phone books, cell phones, or computers.

- Visit local seniors in your community. Spend time with them, make crafts, play games, share stories, or help them with their housework and errands.

- Organize a sporting event for kids with disabilities. Call Dreams for Kids for more ideas or check our Extreme Recess schedule to volunteer.

- Spend time with at-risk kids. Tutor them, read with them, and help them with their homework and job searches.

- There are many fun and easy ways to raise money for struggling nonprofits. Organize a 5K Walk/Run. Host an after work party or business networking event and donate the admission fee. Join a sponsored service day, such as the Dreams for Kids 10 Campaign. Clean out your attic; list unused items on eBay or organize a group garage sale with your neighbors.

- Think global, act local. Gather a group of your friends and choose a global issue. Connect with a family in a developing country. Share culture and ask how you can empower and transform their lives. Contact Dreams for Kids for assistance.

- Host a dinner party and invite a nonprofit leader to join your friends to share the organization's mission.

- For even more ideas visit www.dreamsforkids.org/ways-help

You Can Make a Difference Now!

Dreams for Kids is a registered, nonprofit 501(c) (3) charity. Our local and global programs depend on the engagement of volunteers and the financial support of individuals, business sponsorships, and employee-giving programs. There are many ways you can be involved and help empower a generation of youth.

Contact us, today!

Name _____

Address _____

City _____

State _____ Zip code _____

Country _____

Cell Phone _____

Email _____

I want to make a difference!

Contact me regarding the following:

___ Volunteer Opportunities   ___ Fundraising Opportunities

___ Dream Leaders Program   ___ Extreme Recess

___ Holiday for Hope   ___ Overseas Trips

___ Employee Giving Plans   ___ Sponsorship Opportunities

___ Planned Giving   ___ 10 Campaign

Dreams for Kids, Inc.

155 N. Michigan Avenue, Suite 700, Chicago, Illinois 60601
1-866-729-5454
www.dreamsforkids.org

Your contribution is tax deductible.

Thank you!

Letters from Readers

"If I write so much, my words may let me down. The book *Dreams for Kids* is now a treasure, shared with everyone, and those who have been so inspired that the next thing they do is to get up and start making a difference! It's true. We need to remind ourselves everyday that we have something to give. Your wise and inspirational words have guided me through the dark times. *Dreams for Kids* is a dream come true on its own."

— Tendai, South Africa

"I am still so touched by your book, *Dreams for Kids*, and watching as others become touched. My mom called yesterday to say she can't put the book down. Your story has changed my life—the inspiration I found in the "power of one" triggered a realization that I want to dedicate my life to kids. I'm now in the discovery process of looking into becoming a clinical child psychologist, with the intention of specializing in kids who are sick or live with disabilities. I can't thank you enough for bringing clarity to my life."

— K.D., Chicago, Ill

"Wow, Wow, WOW!!! Your energy just flows off the page and into this reader's inspiration center! The way that your path merged with the heroes and heroines in your book is amazing! And it just confirms that one life touches another by divine order and not by coincidence! We are always striving for awareness and, beyond that, the real challenge—true social inclusion... Thank you for writing such an inspirational book. I will pass it along to my family and friends. Take care."

— D.L., New Jersey

"I finished reading *Dreams for Kids*—the most inspirational book I have ever read...Your style is honest and to the point and immediately connects people. These were the most absolutely amazing and inspirational people. This book is so heartfelt and real. I walk away with a fuller sense of commitment to helping others. This book took me through a range of emotions—I don't cry easily and I tried to hold my composure, but I found that 5 or 6 times on the beach, I had tears uncontrollably streaming down my cheeks (while hiding it from my wife) due to the higher place you brought me. Thank you for your "blue print"—I want to spread your message and have all of my family members and friends read this powerful book."

— L.H., Chicago, Ill

"*Dreams for Kids* is the greatest gift of my life. The book continues to inspire, motivate, and enrich my dream of serving disadvantaged and hopeless children in my community. For me, this book truly means that each of us has a potential in us and, by unleashing the potential, we can make a difference in other lives. Many thanks for your creativity and the true heart and love you have for the disadvantaged and hopeless children around the world. You have demonstrated this by writing this book, which is now spreading around the world. May Almighty God Bless You."

— R.O., Uganda

"I enjoyed *Dreams for Kids* so much. I couldn't put it down. From the start, with J.J.'s story (I was in a heap) and all of the other stories and people you wrote about, the book was so inspiring. It's just amazing to me how you get it so well. You really seem to understand the nature, the mindset, and the frustrations of a special needs person and those who take care of them. I never really put a word to it, but it is isolation that we feel. There was just so much in the book that I could personally relate to and so many inspiring words that I want to remember. I plan to read it again, a little slower, with a highlighter, so I can be sure to remember it all."

— T.S., DuPage, Ill

"I feel as if I have been swept up into a magical world where miracles happen and dreams come true. *Dreams for Kids* is so superbly written and has inspired me to be a better person—a dolphin that senses need and jumps into unchartered waters without even being asked and without concern for the consequences—just for the chance to change someone else's life for the better.

Your book has made me reassess where true joy comes from—the joy of giving my heart, mind, and soul to help someone less fortunate.

I was so empowered by reading the stories of the unimaginable courage of the people in this book, and their cycle of giving and gratitude, giving back what has been so freely given to them. If they can do it, is there any excuse for the rest of us?"

— H.S., Oakland, CA

"It is 2:20 a.m. I remember seeing GHOSTS at Stratford, Ontario, years ago. Twelve hundred people exited the theatre in silence. It was an extraordinary thing to be part of. Your book gave me a repeat experience. Yet this time I was alone. I feel that a tremendous wave of peace has filled my being. I sense a powerful clarity about what my tomorrows will be, without a clue of how they will unfold. *Dreams for Kids* is remarkable. Your voice, your words, your story-telling, is unreal. Such power and simplicity. There are not words enough to adequately define my reactions and feelings."

— J.O., Skokie, Ill

Acknowledgments

If I have seen further, it is by standing on the shoulders of Giants.

~ Isaac Newton

My life has been graced by giants. I have paid tribute to many of them in this book. For all the other giants who have blessed my life, I acknowledge and thank each of you for being the difference in my life.

It is clear to me, as Tennyson said, "I am a part of all that I have met." It is equally clear that Dreams for Kids is the sum total of every single person who has contributed to its growth. If a single person was removed from the history of Dreams for Kids, or from my life, it is unimaginable all this would exist, or I would have lived such a fortunate life.

My family; Michael, Tress, Barrett, Kealan, Adam, Jim, Maureen, Brendan, Liam, Tara, Seamus, Kathleen, and Heather, are the legacy of an extraordinary women. I am grateful for each of you. Long live the love of Patricia Tuohy.

Thank you to the Dreams for Kids staff, interns, and members of our Executive and Associate Boards, who have given their time and their hearts, and helped to make Dreams for Kids the world changing organization that it is—this is your legacy.

A special thank you to the incomparable Shelly Gonsch, for your 21 years of dedication, loyalty and support—it has made all the difference for Dreams for Kids, and for me.

A book only comes to life with a team. I am grateful to Sam Horn, for taking that chair, and to Andrew Horn, for his DC dream. I am in debt to Kristen DeRosa, Catherine O'Connell, Steve Pontikes, Marty Zei, Andrea Patten, Devyani Seth, and Ryan Turek, for your generous contributions of time, talent and honesty.

Thank you to the Chicago Blackhawks for believing in this dream in the very beginning, and to Rocky Wirtz, Lizzy Queen, and Pete Hassen, for your extraordinary partnership.

Dreams for Kids has been blessed with an amazing group of professionals who are paying forward their time and resources to advance our mission in immeasurable ways, including Chapman and Cutler, Dick Thomas and the Tris3ct team, Brandon Jung and our IBM team, Nancy Keres, Mitch Apley and the team of RDS Chicago, Niko Drakoulis and the Akoo team, Doug Plank and the Mobile Cause team, Mark Barnes and Dave Lawless of Designed Plastics, Dave Dipple of Maximum Printing, IBEW Local #134, Athletico, Grainger, Margaret Kielb of Light Bay Studio, and Gregg Sherkin of Oprah's Angel Network.

Thank you to John Ferrentino, Ken Pino, and Mike Caddigan, for being our guys when we really needed you.

Special thanks to Jeffrey Ortmann, A.J. Peterson, Professor Brian Sternthal, Jeffrey Ernstoff, Jim Hayhurst and his Dreambirds, Bill Nolan, Maribeth Browne, Frank Martusciello, Erika Wright, Ron Rispoli and ICRE, Jim Elliott and Diveheart, Ted Devine and 1 World Sports, Chicago Bears, Pierre Thomas, Vince Calabrese, Triecia Dolan, Kyree Gerson, Abby Kritzler, Vivian Hapaniewski, Billy McFall, Hillard Heintze, LLC, United States Marine Corps, and for the marketing brilliance and generosity of Matthew Bennett of BTDT.

Kevin McFarland, thank you for bringing humanity to the most desperate places on earth, for your invaluable counsel and friendship to me, and for introducing Dreams for Kids to the world.

Rob and Ada Wolcott, thank you for your friendship, and for sharing your KIN vision to change our world.

In a life rich with great friendship, I have had more amazing friends than one person deserves. Thank you, Shawn Warner, for your unconditional loyalty and support. Michael Palmieri and John Carter, my amigos, I am eternally grateful to you both for holding me accountable.

With gratitude in my heart, I honor the memory of Joe Lagattuta, who knew when a young kid needed a father figure, and I thank his son Nick, who never gave up on that kid when he needed a friend.

For the Lawless clan—"Here's to Jeff."

To all my heroes at ICRE and Harlan—the world has heard you. You will never be forgotten.

To every kid who is waiting—never lose hope. Always believe in the possibilities of your life, and your rightful place in the history of the world.

About the Author

Tom Tuohy is Founder and President of Dreams for Kids.

Tom is a graduate of DePaul University. While attending DePaul Law School, Tom studied at Cambridge University in England and returned to DePaul to receive his Juris Doctorate. He is currently enrolled in Northwestern University's Kellogg School Executive Scholars Program.

Tom founded Tuohy Law Offices and concentrated in a career which provided legal education seminars to municipal employees, members of labor unions, and the general public.

Inspired by his mother, Tom founded Dreams for Kids in 1989.

Tom has been recognized by several organizations for his work on behalf of children and sits on several non profit boards. He speaks extensively to business organizations, labor unions, student groups and educators.

Tom has learned in over 20 years of Dreams for Kids, that every person can make an extraordinary difference, every child deserves the opportunity to lead, serve, and fearlessly pursue their dreams, and we all can compassionately change the world.

Tom was born in Chicago and lives in Park Ridge, Illinois.

Take Action Plan

I am only one, but I am one. I cannot do everything, but I can do something. And I will not let what I cannot do interfere with what I can do.
~ Edward Everett Hale

Change begins with us. We must be the change we seek. This is the most exciting and promising time in history. Together, we can change the world. I look forward to working with you to meet our greatest challenge, and to empower a generation whose time has come. Today is our day to act. Plan how you wish to engage. The following pages are provided for your notes and your action plan.

Act boldly! Make an extraordinary difference!

_____

_____

_____

_____

_____

_____

_____

One person can make a difference and create lasting change in the world. Your impact on a single person can result in a ripple effect felt far and wide.

This is the true story of Dreams for Kids. It is a story of hope, empowerment, and transformation.

During one of the most challenging times in human history, when so many people are seeking a sense of fulfillment and a reason to hope, this book gives you the inspiration you need to act and do your part...one person at a time.

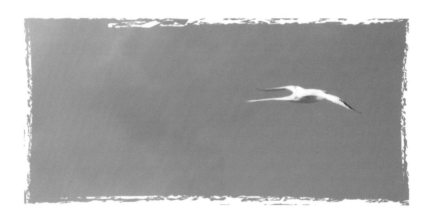

"*Dreams for Kids is more than a book. It is a compelling yet practical vision for how to live and change the world. You will be inspired and empowered...and it will change your life.*"

Robert C. Wolcott, Ph.D.
Founder & Executive Director, Kellogg Innovation Network,
Kellogg School of Management, Northwestern University

All profits from the sale of this book
will be donated to Dreams for Kids, Inc.

ISBN 978-0615368184

9 780615 368184   51495